SECRET CHELMSFORD

Jim Reeve

AMBERLEY

First published 2016

Amberley Publishing
The Hill, Stroud
Gloucestershire, GL5 4EP

www.amberley-books.com

Copyright © Jim Reeve, 2016

The right of Jim Reeve to be identified as the Author
of this work has been asserted in accordance with the
Copyrights, Designs and Patents Act 1988.

ISBN 978 1 4456 5035 7 (print)
ISBN 978 1 4456 5036 4 (ebook)

British Library Cataloguing in Publication Data.
A catalogue record for this book is available from the
British Library.

Typesetting by Amberley Publishing.
Printed in Great Britain.

Contents

Introduction

Chelmsford is a fascinating city and hides many secrets among its infrastructure and population. Who could guess that under Asda's car park lies a Neolithic cursus and burial mound, or that a sword factory is now spending eternity beneath Parkway car park.

At first the Romans did not settle in the city but Boudicca (also spelt Boudicea), Queen of the Iceni, was responsible for changing that after her uprising in AD 60/61. What remains of a mansio (a place where Roman dignitaries could stay for the night) lies under the modern Moulsham, and when you drive round the Odeon roundabout, you are driving over the remains of a Roman temple.

The Romans established a military post on the road from London to Colchester. The fort soon expanded, giving the troops some comfort with bath houses and a market. The Romans named it *Caesaromagus* (meaning Caesar's Field) and it is the only town to bear the name of Caesar.

When the Vandals sacked Rome in AD 410 the Romans called their troops back to defend the homeland. Chelmsford and the rest of Britain sank into the Dark Ages and all that the Romans had built began to fall into disrepair. The bridge that the Romans built over the Can collapsed but there was a ford, controlled by a Saxon called Ceolmaer. It was he who gave his name to Chelmsford. Another Saxon name was given to Moulsham: The Muls Ham, the home of Mul.

There was a settlement to the north of the present city centre by the time the Normans invaded in 1066. When William the Conqueror ordered the Domesday Book in 1086 the manor of Chelmsford was described as 'a small rural farm which contained four families'. The other half of Chelmsford, Moulsham, was recorded as having twelve families. This area of the city is where it is thought its roots were planted.

In the twelfth century a bridge was built over the river Can which followed the old Roman road from London to Colchester. Bad King John, who ruled from 1199–1216, visited Chelmsford on 21 March 1201 on his journey from London to York, and granted William of Sainte-Mere-Eglise, the Bishop of London, the right to hold a three-day annual fair in the High Street commencing on 1 May. The charter allowed the bishop to make money for the church by selling plots in the market place. Entrepreneurs of the day, who included some French men, took this opportunity and made money from the travellers on their way from London to Colchester, via the old Roman Road, which passed through Chelmsford. The bishop charged an annual fee for the privilege. The cheapest plots were narrower and were down towards the river. The more expensive ones were as long as 600 feet. The buyers could sell them on, provided they had permission from the bishop and, no doubt, at a fee. Gradually, as time went on more permanent buildings were erected. From the fourteenth century onwards a channel was cut down the centre of the High Road which discharged water into the river, carrying all the waste from the animals and rubbish with it, which

Shire Hall, around the 1900s.

The Market Place, around 1910. (Copright Chelmsford Museum)

caused pollution. At that time the town's main public water supply was a spring-fed conduit, which came from Burgeyswell to the town centre through underground pipes. Following an outbreak of cholera in 1850, the board of health appointed Edward Cresy to investigate and report to them on Chelmsford's sanitation problems. Following the report, James Fenton was asked to produce plans for a healthy water supply and sewerage system. Thanks to Fenton, today, Chelmsford is a good place to live and work.

DID YOU KNOW THAT...?

England was governed from Chelmsford during the period 1 July 1381 to 6 July 1381. After the Peasants' Revolt, Richard II visited the city. From here he sent out orders to the rest of the kingdom. Many of the leaders of the revolt were executed on Primrose Hill.

DID YOU KNOW THAT...?

Chelmsford has been the county town of Essex since 1215, which was the same year as the Magna Carta was signed.

The population of Chelmsford rose by 10,552 from the census in 2001 to the one held in 2011. In 2001 the female population amounted to 50.8 per cent and the male to 49.2 per cent.

Law and Order

On the Beat

Under Fifty Nine restaurant, down in the basement, there are stark police cells. The walls have smooth, white tiles. It is reported that there is a passage which leads through to the magistrates court in Shire Hall. The idea was that prisoners could be taken through to the court without the risk of escape.

Before the County Police Act of 1830 was implemented in Chelmsford, night-watchmen patrolled the streets trying to ensure that crime was kept to a minimum. Night-watchmen had their origins back in Greek and Roman times. It was Henry III (1216–72) who brought in a law requiring the appointment of watchmen. The Assizes of Arms required the appointment of constables to prevent and stop any breaches of the peace and to arrest anyone who had committed a crime and take them before the sheriff. Later, in 1252 he decreed that every city and borough should appoint between six and twelve men, according to the number of citizens, to watch through the night. The watchman's role was to patrol the streets at night, calling out the hour, checking properties and ensuring there were no disturbances. By 1820 crime had risen and continued to rise, so that in 1839 the government was eventually forced to bring in the County Police Act.

By the following year Essex had implemented the act and formed the Essex Police Force. Constables had four weeks' training and were then required to work a seven-day week, walking up to 20 miles a day. While on duty they had no breaks and were expected to eat while working. They were paid the same as a farm labourer, £1 10s a week, despite the fact that often their lives were at risk. Discipline was very strict and if caught off their beat, asleep or drunk they could be fined or sacked. Their only means of communication was a whistle, which was not a lot of good if they were miles out in the countryside. They were often assaulted and occasionally killed, as in the case of Sergeant Evans, who came across a gang trying to steal wheat from a farm. He tackled them but they cut his throat. The three men involved were caught and the ringleader, John Davis, was hanged from the gate at Springfield Prison in front of thousands of people who came to watch. The public raised £40 for Sergeant Evans' widow, and the police gave her a pension of £15 a year.

The first chief constable, Capt. John McHardy, was selected from nineteen candidates. As an ex-navy officer, he was very good at organizing. He soon created links with Colchester and ensured his recruits could read, write and were fit and honest. In 1840 the number in the force rose to 115 and he had to manage on a budget of £10,000. Some people thought that the police were a waste of money. Kent was one of those counties that at first decided against setting up a police force. They studied crime in London, before and after Sir Robert Peel set up the Metropolitan Police Force, and concluded that as crime had increased they would not implement the act.

The original Chelmsford police station.

Old police cells.

The first chief constable of Essex, John McHardy.

A female police constable in the early days.

The old prison gate, around the turn of the twentieth century.

During his time in office, Chief Constable McHardy introduced a merit medal for outstanding conduct. Ten sergeants and twenty constables received the medal, and in the case of the sergeants they also received an additional 2s a week. The constables were awarded an extra shilling.

Today the Essex police have 3,600 officers and it is one of the largest forces outside the Metropolitan Police Force. The county has a population of 1.6 million and covers 1,400 square miles. Sadly, since 1849, fourteen officers have been killed in the line of duty. A special branch was set up in 1970 to deal with terrorists and anything that may affect life or property internally or nationally. Their workload increased considerably following the 9/11 attacks.

Lock Them Up

The first prisons in Chelmsford were built in 1658 by the side of where the Stone Bridge is today. Being by the side of the river the buildings were prone to dampness and subsidence, which enabled one prisoner to dig his way out of the decaying walls with a stick. Another inmate, who had only one hand, decided it would be easier just to walk out.

There were two jails, one behind the other. One was for petty crimes, such as prostitution and fraud, and was meant to give a short sharp shock to the prisoners, and sentences were normally only two to three weeks. The second prison was for more serious offences like murder, robbery and for stealing a man's tools of his trade. Prisoners in this prison had longer sentences, were transported, or hanged.

The prisons became so dilapidated it was realised that something had to be done. It was decided to build a new brick prison at Springfield and building started in 1822. It was designed to accommodate 275 prisoners in 214 cells; forty were set aside for women. As the old prisons were demolished their inhabitants were transferred to the new one. Soon Springfield became overcrowded and prisoners were forced to sleep in corridors, cupboards or anywhere the prison authorities could find a space.

When prisoners were allocated a cell, they were given two blankets each and had to sleep on stone beds. Even in the depths of winter there was no heating and prisoners shivered under their blankets. Part of the prison was set aside for boys, who could be as young as eight. These youngsters were subjected to a very strict regime, which often meant being beaten with the birch, receiving as many as fifty strokes. Men were given the cat-o-nine-tails, which was a whip with lead on the end of its nine leather thongs. The whip could strip the flesh to the bone and frequently did. The prison did accommodate a number of women, but they were not subjected to the same punishment as the men.

Soon after the prison was opened life became even harder when the treadmill was introduced. Both sexes were forced to walk on the wheel for up to ten hours a day. Eventually, this cruel punishment was stopped for women.

Once a month prisoners were allowed a bath in the open prison yard, even in winter with frost and snow on the ground (and one assumes in cold water). It is a wonder that any of them survived on the rations they were given; $1^{1}/_{2}$ pounds of bread and 2 pints of beer a day, but no vegetables. The beer was stopped in 1834. After prisoners had served three months their relations were allowed to bring food in, and the food allowance was increased to include onions and 1 pint of soup three times a week.

The walls of the prison were 28 feet high. There was a chapel and an infirmary. Sentences were normally up to three months or else prisoners were transported or, if they were unlucky, hanged.

The idea of separate accommodation for male and female prisoners came about after the Peel Act of 1823. The act dictated that women prisoners should be supervised by matrons and female warders only. During the eighteenth century it was discovered that in Moulsham Prison female and male prisoners were not separated in hospital and a fine of £500 was imposed. In 1860 it was agreed to build a separate infirmary for women at Springfield Prison. Rosetta Petchey, who was only nineteen, gave the *Essex Weekly News* her account of spending three months in prison. She said she had to be up by 6.30 a.m. and at 6.40 a.m., a wardress lit the gaslight and made sure she was up. Then she was expected to clean her cell and chamber pot. Breakfast was eaten in her cell at 7.30 a.m. and consisted of gruel and 6 ounces of barley bread. After breakfast she had to attend a church service which was followed by walking round the exercise yard for an hour. She then started work on picking rope-yarn or washing in her cell. Prisoners were not allowed to talk to one another and if they were caught they were severely punished. At midday she broke for dinner, which consisted, on Wednesdays and Sundays, of 6 ounces of bread and potatoes. On two other days of the week she had ½ pint of soup and 6 ounces of bread. The rest of the week she had gruel. After dinner she was locked in her cell to work until 5.20 p.m. The evening meal was gruel and bread again. The number of female prisoners jailed during 1891 was 221, and during the same period 1,917 men were imprisoned. The cost for keeping a prisoner for a year was £12.6s 8d.

Capt. Thomas Neal, the first governor of Springfield Prison.

The first governor of Springfield Prison was Thomas Neal, who not only managed the prison but was responsible for the setting up of Chelmsford's Museum.

William Cooper was a 'trustee' in the prison and was allowed to use a ladder to light the prison lights while being watched by a warder. One day the ladder was left lying about, and so trusty taking advantage of the situation, William climbed the ladder and slipped over the wall, evading capture for over a year. One of the most famous prisoners held in Springfield Prison until he escaped was Alfred George Hinds, who had escaped on two other occasions after having been sentenced in 1953 to twelve years for jewel theft. He went to live in Ireland until he was captured. He made thirteen appeals against his conviction and was finally pardoned.

The prison at one time housed debtors, but they were not subjected to the same strict regime. No doubt you know that Springfield has been seen worldwide on television in the very successful series *Porridge*, which starred Ronnie Barker and was filmed at the jail in 1979. The Sex Pistols did a live performance in 1976. The prison today is a young persons' institution and can hold 740 prisoners.

The prison is supposed to be haunted by a mother and her four children. The second governor of the prison, Capt. McGormy, had four children but all died before they were eleven. Then, suddenly his wife died. Soon after, warders and prisoners started hearing the voices of children and seeing a crimson-bonneted lady walking through the corridors.

Hang Them High

It is difficult to believe that men, women and youths as young as seventeen were hanged over the front entrance of Springfield Prison. The original gate, which was the porter's lodge, had a flat roof strong enough to support the scaffold. On a day that there was to be a hanging, the citizens of Chelmsford would gather in their thousands in the grounds outside. It was recorded that when, on the 14 August, 1848, Mary May was executed for the murder of her brother, 3,000 spectators watched. At the executions, refreshment stalls were set up, trinkets were sold and, after the hanging, the executioner would cut up the rope and sell it piece by piece.

The first man to be hanged over the prison gate was James Winter, who was hanged on the 10 December, 1827. He had murdered Thomas Patrick, the landlord of the Yorkshire Grey, a public house in Colchester, who had accused him of robbing a man at a sale. Over the years, forty men and two women followed him up the stairs to their appointment with the hangman. Charles Fremd, a seventy-one-year-old German, was the last man to be hanged. His execution took place on the 4 November 1914. He was convicted of murdering his wife, by slitting her throat. In desperation he tried to cut his own, but failed. The hangman made no such mistake. He was the oldest man and the last to be hanged at Springfield Prison.

Thirty of the forty-three prisoners at Springfield were hanged for murder: two for assault, five for arson, two for horse stealing, one for rape, one for robbery, one for an unnatural crime and one for highway robbery. The youngest criminal to be hanged was sixteen-year-old James Cook on the 27 March 1829 for arson. He worked as a cowman and had set fire to premises belonging to his employer, William Green.

The most unfortunate wife of a prisoner must have been Mrs Turner. Her husband John and his gang were convicted for robbery of a property in Grays. He was hanged but his gang, although convicted and sentenced to death, were at the last moment reprieved. John Turner's widow married a Mr Passfield, who was later convicted of arson at the Lent Assizes, and was hanged in Springfield.

Hangmen each had a preference for the length of rope they used. A short rope meant the prisoner was strangled to death and took ages to die; often they were helped by the hangman swinging on the prisoner's legs. The most famous for this type of hanging was William Calcraft, who served as public hangman from 1829 to 1874. He was a local man, born in Little Baddow, Essex in 1800. It is believed that he used the short rope so that he could entertain the crowd. He also administered the cat-o-nine-tails to adult men and the birch to youngsters. He carried out his trade all over the country and only carried one bag of luggage to an execution. This contained the implements of his trade: a new rope, a white hood to place over the prisoner's head, and straps to pin back his arms. Although many people hated his methods of execution, he was very popular and was often greeted like royalty. Calcraft carried out the last hanging open to the public and the first private one held inside a prison after the passing of the Criminal Punishment Amendment Act of 1869.

DID YOU KNOW THAT...?

The army took over the prison soon after the First World War when it started to house army prisoners. The prison only reverted to a civilian one in 1931.

Pierrepoint was the next best known hangman who, it is believed, carried out between 400 to 600 executions, but nobody really knows as no records were kept. Pierrepoint was very popular because he was efficient and carried out the hanging with no fuss. He was born in 1905 in Yorkshire and worked as a greengrocer. He carried out the executions to earn extra money. He used the long rope method, as opposed to Calcraft's short rope, and therefore the fall through the trapdoor broke the prisoners' necks as opposed to strangling them.

Pierrepoint was responsible for dispatching a number of notorious criminals, including the well-known traitor during the Second World War, Lord Haw-Haw (as William Joyce was known when he broadcasted from Germany). Pierrepoint carried out the last hanging of a woman in 1955. Ruth Ellis shot her lover David Blakely after a stormy affair and was hanged in Holloway prison for her crime.

He fell out with the local authority when they would not pay him as the prisoner was reprieved at the last moment. Pierrepoint argued that he had travelled to the prison and had incurred costs, but they refused to pay him. When Pierrepoint retired he wrote a book about his experiences.

The last hangings took place in 1964, when Gwynne Evans, aged twenty-four, was hanged at Strangeways Prison while his partner in crime, Peter Allen, aged twenty-one, was hanged in Walton Prison for bludgeoning to death John West, for the paltry sum of 10 pounds. Peter Allen's wife visited him before he was executed and in the reception room Allen lost his temper and smashed the safety glass that separated them. They were unlucky because a few months later when Labour came to power they suspended the death sentence for murder and changed the law a year later, in 1965.

DID YOU KNOW THAT...?

There was never a government-appointed hangman. Each local authority was free to choose whoever they wanted.

DID YOU KNOW THAT...?

William Calcraft was paid a weekly wage of a guinea and another when he hanged someone. To earn extra money he would cut the execution rope up and sell it.

When the Nuremberg Trial finally concluded Pierrepoint was selected to hang forty of the war crime criminals who had been involved with the extermination of the Jews.

Your Money or Your Life

One of the most famous gangs that went on trial in Chelmsford Assizes was the Coggeshall Gang, who consisted of fourteen ruthless members. Between 1844 and 1848 they terrified the Coggeshall area. Samuel Crow planned their robberies and was the leader of the gang. Their hideaway was the Black Horse, which was owned by Crow's half- brother William French, who acted as their fence. The Essex police had been formed for only four years when the gang began their criminal activities and they had great difficulty in arresting them. The Witham division, where the gang operated, was staffed by a superintendent and four constables. Samuel Crow, the leader of the gang, was a post-chaise driver and used the knowledge he gained ferrying people around to farms and large houses to plan his robberies.

The first property they burgled was unoccupied and the only valuable found was the wine cellar, the proceeds of which they no doubt drank and sold in the Black Horse. In fear of the police uncovering their crime, the gang set fire to the house. The break-ins continued with one at The Bird in Hand public house and a number of other properties in the district. The population was terrified, especially when the news of their worst crime got out. Four of the gang broke into Mr Finch's house and tortured him and his housekeeper for hours, trying to make them reveal where their money was hidden. They suspended the housekeeper over the open fire until she was badly burned. She screamed and struggled until her clothes caught fire. Only then did they cut her down. Despite her pain, she did not reveal where the money was. They then turned their attention on to Mr French. They dragged him up the stairs and threw a rope over a beam, in an upstairs room and hauled him up. When he was half dead, they cut him down.

In the same year they piled furniture on top of another man, trying to get him to reveal and only stopped when they thought they had killed him. In 1848, the gang's luck ran out when William Wade was caught and was sentenced to transportation for fifteen years. While he was waiting for a sailing date, in Chelmsford Prison Sam Crow, the leader of the gang, visited him and promised that if Wade did not squeal on the rest of the gang he would look after his family. Before he was transported, Wade found out that his family was suffering and that Sam Crow had gone back on his word. Wade asked to see the governor and gave him the names of the rest of the gang. One by one, the gang was captured. Finally, the police found Samuel Crow sitting on a beam in the roof of the Black Horse. Breathing a sigh of relief that they had finally cornered him, the police rushed at him, but he climbed out onto the roof and escaped by jumping down onto a cart that his fifteen-year-old brother had brought up. Before the police could recapture him, the brother whipped up the horses and drove off to a local

Statue of Judge Tindal.

mill, where Crow hid. No doubt Crow had planned his escape long before, as the cart was owned by Crow's half-brother, William French. Crow made his way to London and decided to flee to Germany. Crow must have breathed a sigh of relief as he boarded the boat, but just as he thought he was safe he was confronted by two police officers who had seen his picture in the *Police Gazette*. At his trial in March 1849 the courtroom was crowded. Two other members of the gang, Tansley and Ellis, were put on trial with him. The judge considered sentencing Crow to death, but in the end sentenced him to be transported for life to Australia. He escaped justice by dying in Chelmsford Prison before the ship sailed. Two other members of the gang and the fifteen-year-old John Crow were sentenced to seven years transportation.

Trial by Combat

Can you imagine the shock on the jury's faces when the prisoner in the dock slowly took off his leather gauntlet and, narrowing his eyes, hurled it to the floor at the feet of the youth challenging him, to trial by combat? The teenager was accusing him of murdering his sister. By doing so, Thornton evoked an old English law that had never been repealed. The year was 1817 and the case was being presided over by the famous Judge Tindal, who was born in Chelmsford. The unusual case of Ashford v. Thornton came before him as the result of an appeal by the victim's teenaged brother. At an earlier trial it had been alleged that Thornton had murdered Mary Ashford after meeting her at a dance, and that they had wandered off into the night and had intercourse. Next morning she was found lying in a pond, face down.

At his original trial, Thornton produced witnesses to say that he had been nowhere near the pond that night and therefore could not have committed the murder. The jury returned a verdict of not guilty.

Mary Ashford's young brother was not satisfied with the verdict and appealed against it. Thornton was brought back to court before Judge Tindal. As he stood in the dock, Thornton must have slowly pulled off his glove and hurled it down at the feet of Mary Ashford's brother and challenged him to trial by combat. The brother looked at the glove for a moment and then, at Thornton, who was much bigger than him, and wisely decided not to accept the challenge. Judge Tindal dismissed the case.

The act of trial by combat was originally implemented in Germany and is thought to have been brought to England by William the Conqueror. The first recorded case in England was Wulfstan v. Walter. The law was repealed in 1818, a year after the trial of Mr Thornton.

Judge Tindal was one of the most famous judges of the eighteenth century and was brought up at No. 199 Moulsham Street, Chelmsford, and educated at King Edward VI Grammar School and then continued his education at Trinity College, Cambridge. He presided over a number of famous cases, the most notable of these being when George IV accused his wife, Queen Caroline of Brunswick, of having an affair with an Italian, Bartolomeo Pergami, who was the Queen's servant. George and his wife never got on, which was not really surprising. His father had forced him to marry her in exchange for clearing his gambling debts and they had never met before the wedding. On top of that, the King declared she never bathed and so smelled. George claimed that he had sex with her only when he was drunk and that it had been only on three occasions – twice on the first night and once on the second. From one of those couplings they had their daughter, Princess Charlotte. It was also alleged that George had secretly married Maria Fitzherbert before his marriage to Caroline. Apparently, he carried on the liaison with her for years.

In 1814, the King and Caroline separated and she moved to Italy where it was alleged she started having an affair with her Italian servant Bartolomeo Pergami. The Queen returned to England to answer the accusations. Being very popular, crowds gathered outside the court to support her. Tindal defended her and the case was dismissed.

Many an insane prisoner has Judge Tindal to thank for bringing in the law of 'Not guilty by reason of insanity'. Daniel M'Naghten fired at who he thought was Sir Robert Peel, but instead shot his secretary, Mr Drummond. As it was only a flesh wound, Mr Drummond was able to walk away but, within five days, he was dead. Mr M'Naghten was charged with his murder. The trial commenced on the 2 March 1843, and the defence argued that Mr Drummond had died not as a result of the shot wound but of the doctors having bled him. It was further argued that M'Naghten suffered from delusions of persecution and the defence asked for a verdict of 'Not guilty by reason of insanity'. The jury agreed and Mr M'Naghten was put in a mental institution.

Another famous case where Judge Tindal changed the law was in the case of Rex v. Hale. It was a trial following the Bristol riots when a man was shot and killed. Judge Tindal thought Mr Hale had been so provoked that any reasonable man would have reacted in the same way and directed the jury to bring in a verdict of manslaughter.

After his time in the law, Judge Tindal decided to go into politics and became the Tory MP for Wigtown in Scotland, and then Harwich. He later became the solicitor general.

The site where Judge Tindal was born, now Lloyds Bank.

Threadneedle Street fire station around 1914. (Copyright Essex Fire Brigade)

Chelmsford Fire Brigade

Nicholas Barbon was responsible for planting the roots of the fire brigade following the Great Fire of London in 1666. He had trained in the medical profession and became an honorary fellow of the Royal College of Physicians, but saw a financial opportunity after the fire and turned to the building trade. It did not take him long to become one of the most prominent builders in London. Between 1680 and 1681 he and some associates set up an insurance company, which offered fire insurance to 5,000 properties in London. There was a plate on the front of the buildings insured by them, in order that the fire brigade could identify those buildings that were covered by insurance and put out any fires. Those uninsured were left to their own devices to put out the flames.

Prior to Nicholas Barbon setting up his company, it was the case of the individual doing the best he or she could with a handpump and buckets of water. Edinburgh was the first city to set up a fire brigade – in 1823. This was followed by a number of London companies

Market Street fire station. (Copyright Essex Fire Brigade)

merging and becoming The London Fire Engine Establishment. Gradually, the primitive equipment was replaced with steam pumps. There were over 1,000 different fire brigades over the country and, with the Second World War on the horizon, the National Fire Service was established in 1938.

DID YOU KNOW THAT...?

The Chelmsford Fire Brigade had a station in Market Street opposite Threadneedle Street. It was vacated in 1950 when it moved to Springfield Road and then finally to Rainsford Lane around 1959.

Above left: The type of fire tender used in around 1758.

Above right: The Stone Bridge, built in 1787.

Places of Interest

The Crunch of Marching Feet

The stone bridge which spans the River Can has always proved to be fascinating. It was opened in 1788, although the keystone is dated 1787. It is not difficult to imagine the number of feet that have trodden its length, from those of soldiers marching down to Harwich to fight in the Napoleonic Wars, to modern-day shoppers. At one time during the Napoleonic Wars there were more troops in Chelmsford than citizens.

The original bridge, which joins Chelmsford and Moulsham, was built in 1199 and provided an important route from London to Colchester. It lasted until 1372, when a new one had to be constructed. This replacement surprisingly lasted until 1761 when it became dangerous. To alleviate the situation, a foot bridge of wood was constructed, but within twenty-three years that too had become dangerous. The magistrates of the town decided it was time to invest in a new bridge that would last for centuries. It was designed by the surveyor James Johnson, and he proposed a bridge of one span measuring 34 feet. The problem was that the river was 54 feet wide and so they had to reduce its width. Unfortunately, nobody foresaw that this would cause flooding. A number of materials for the bridge were suggested, including Thomas Telford's proposal of constructing it of iron, but eventually the stone bridge we have today was decided upon, proving that the right decision was taken at that time.

During its long life one of the balusters fell into the river and was left there until 1960, when it was located during some flood-relief work and restored to its rightful place.

George Eagles was hanged, drawn and quartered on the old bridge for heresy. He was nicknamed 'Trudeover' because he tramped the countryside to avoid capture while preaching the Protestant faith, which was against bloody Queen Mary's laws. Mary ruled England for five long, gory years from 1553 to 1558. At first he managed to evade capture and roamed the country preaching, then a reward was offered and he was finally captured in Colchester. He was dragged to London for trial, where he was found guilty and sentenced to death. He was transported to Chelmsford to meet his grizzly end on the old bridge.

The bridge divides the town neatly into Chelmsford and Moulsham. There was a Roman settlement on the south side of the river but the north side, having been granted a charter to hold a market by King John (1199–1216), grew rich, Moulsham becoming the poor relation.

Caesar's Field

Under the city of Chelmsford lies a Roman town of *Caesaromagus*, which lay on the road to the west of the crossing of the Rivers Cam and Chelmer. The Latin name means 'Caesar's Field'. There is a school of thought proposing that a decisive battle was fought on the site

Moulsham Street today.

Above left: Statue of a Roman centurion.

Above right: A French eagle captured at the Battle of Salamanca, 1812. (Courtesy of Chelmsford Museum)

The old Chelmer Mill, New Street, around 1900. (Copyright Marriages)

by Claudius Caesar when he visited Britain for sixteen days in AD 43. The Romans fought the British Army and then marched on unopposed to Colchester. For a time, between AD 160–200, Roman Chelmsford had some earth defences, but these were later flattened.

Roman Chelmsford is mentioned in a number of their records, one of which relates that it is one of many staging posts between London and Carlisle, where Hadrian's Wall lies and another between London and Colchester. The Roman town gradually developed and evidence of Roman occupation of the city has been found, particularly during a dig in 1970. A fourth-century Roman temple was found with various coins, brooches, a bracelet and rings. The diameter of the temple was 36 feet. It was surrounded by a porch that measured 58 feet.

Between Nos 29–31 Rochford Road, a 13-foot-wide Roman road was uncovered. Evidence was also found of first-century cremations and in approximately the same area a stone quarry was found. Between 191 and 192 Moulsham-Street evidence of timber buildings was found and it is thought that they were used as workshops.

When the Vandals sacked Rome in AD 410 the Roman Army was withdrawn and gradually Chelmsford, along with the rest of Britain, slipped into the Dark Ages.

Give Us Our Daily Bread

The mill situated off Parkway, near the Army and Navy roundabout, was built in 1819, but a mill has stood on the site for over 1,000 years and was mentioned in the Domesday Book in 1086. It has been in the ownership of the Marriage family since the seventeenth century when it was established by seventeen-year-old twins.

The mill has seen its share of trouble over the centuries. In 1772 the price of grain had risen so high that people were unable to afford it and were starving. A large crowd decided to storm the mill. Armed with sticks and clubs they attacked the mill and stole sacks of flour. After loading them on carts they took the corn to the marketplace and sold it at a reasonable price. Terrified, the authorities called on the army to put the riot down, but the army refused to move against their own people. In 1815 there was more unrest. At a time when the country should have been celebrating the Battle of Waterloo, the government of the day restricted the import of cheaper corn from America and Russia by imposing tariffs under the Importation Act of 1815. This was brought in by the Conservative government under Prime Minister Robert Jenkinson, the Earl of Liverpool. The Conservatives, who mainly consisted of landowners, wanted to protect their own interest by keeping the price of grain high, while the Wiggs, who were mainly industrialists, opposed the law, which was not repealed until 1845. In those far-off days the labourer mainly lived on bread. It was a time of great social upheaval when many farm labourers moved off the land into the cities for the higher wages manufacturing could give them.

The corn for the Old Moulsham Mill was brought there by horse-pulling barges along the Blackwater and Chelmer Canal. The mill was converted during the nineteenth century from water-powered to steam, which depended on coal brought by the barges. Once the Chelmsford railway became established in 1885, there was no need to use the canal as coal was brought by train and the flour taken to London and then by horse and cart to the various bakers. Until 1950 corn was bought at the corn exchange in Chelmsford.

A new mill was set up by Marriages in New Street, using the new successful system at the old mill. Sadly the old mill was closed in 1972 and then opened in 1983 as a business and craft centre.

The Chelmer Mill today

The old Moulsham Mill in around the 1800s. (Copyright Marriages)

The Old Moulsham Mill today.

Two to One On

Chelmsford did have one of the oldest racecourses in the country. It was believed to have been the only course that circled a church and remains of it can still be seen today. It was said to be a difficult track because the racehorses had to cross the road four times and to gallop uphill to reach the winning post. It is thought that racing was taking place on the track as early as the reign of King Charles II (1660–80) although the earliest recorded meeting was in 1759. In 1764 a three-day meeting was advertised in the *Chelmsford Chronicle* and informed the owners that they had to register their horses at the famous Black Boy Inn, Chelmsford. During the meeting special meals were provided at reduced prices.

The racing venue became even more popular once the railway was built adjacent to Hylands Park because the owners could unload the horses near the track and ride them to the meeting. Racing was not the only entertainment on and around the track. There were prizefights, dogfights and cockfights, games of 'find the lady', eating and drinking tents. Prostitutes and pickpockets toured the grounds, ready to relieve racegoers of their hard-earned winnings. Panic broke out in the stand in 1779 when it burst into flames during the meeting, completely destroying the building. As far as can be established, nobody was injured. The venue was so popular, that it was not long before a new and better stand was built, which held 1,000 racegoers.

During the Napoleonic Wars (1799–1815) batteries of guns were placed in a specially-built fort and earthworks, in order to prevent Napoleon's armies landing at Harwich and marching on London. Luckily they were not needed.

It is recorded that King Edward VII (1841–1910), who was a great gambler, attended the course with all his entourage and must have caused a great commotion among the regular racegoers. During both world wars the course was used as an army training ground. As motoring became popular race meetings impeded the flow of traffic and gradually the track declined.

DID YOU KNOW THAT...?

In 1764 one of the first advertisements in the *Essex Chronicle* was on the horseracing at Galleywood.

DID YOU KNOW THAT...?

Britvic started up in a small chemist shop in Tindal Street selling water-based drinks during the early part of the nineteenth century and was first called the British Vitamin Products Co.

Galleywood Racecourse around 1900.(Copyright Chelmsford Museum)

Approximately where the old Britvic chemist was situated.

Chelmsford at War

The Rebels

In 1381 the peasants were in uproar. They were tied to the land and could not move off a manor without their masters' permission. Wages were low, and following the Black Death prices had risen dramatically. It is true that the plague of 1341 had killed so many workers that those who survived were in great demand and could ask for better conditions. However, conditions were still bad and taxes imposed did not help the situation.

John of Gaunt, the uncle and protector of the fourteen-year-old King Richard II, had imposed a third tax in four years to pay for the war in France. Up until then taxes had only been imposed on landowners, but he came up with the idea for a tax on everyone over fifteen. The first two taxes imposed were 4d and although very difficult for the peasants to pay, they did. The third tax that was imposed was 1s. The landowners could afford it but to the peasants it was a fortune. Admittedly they could pay it in kind – i.e. seeds, animals or even tools – but that meant they had to go hungry.

The rebellion appears to have started in May 1381, in the village of Fobbing, Essex. The taxman Thomas Bampton entered the village and demanded to know why the villagers had not paid their taxes. The inhabitants became angry and threw him out. The authorities then sent in the army, but they were also evicted. At that time, John Bull was going around the country preaching that all men were equal. The saying was, 'When Adam dug and Eve spun who then were the gentlemen?' The protest spread to other parts of the country and the men of Essex and Kent decided to march on London to put their complaints to the King. On the way they attacked and destroyed buildings and any records that recorded the taxes or their serfdom. If any official stood in their way they killed him.

The men from Essex, Suffolk and Norwich converged on St Mary's church in Great Baddow, just outside Chelmsford, under the leadership of Jack Straw. The Kentish men were lead by Watt Tyler. It is thought that he had been a soldier with experience of fighting in France. On their way they attacked Rochester Castle and Canterbury.

On reaching London, the Essex group camped in Mile End and the Kent men camped at Blackheath. At first, the King agreed to see them at Rotherhithe and travelled down the Thames in a barge, but when he saw the massive crowd of 60,000 rebels he panicked and turned back, fearing for his life. The mob became angry at this. Some residents of London deliberately left the city gates open and a band of rebels poured in. Most of the rebels had never travelled more than a few miles from their villages and seeing the temptations of the city, and despite Watt Tyler trying to control them, they went on a rampage, killing many merchants and lawyers. One group broke into Fleet Prison and released the prisoners.

The rebels felt that the taxes were not the fourteen-year-old King's fault but that of his ministers – people such as the Bishop of Canterbury and John of Gaunt. Bravely, Richard agreed to ride out and meet the rebels at Mile End, thereby getting them out of the city. Sitting on his horse, the young King listened to their demands and, trying to placate them, agreed to abolish the poll tax, to set rents at a reasonable level, give peasants a charter of their rights and to pardon the rebels. While the meeting was going on, some of the mob broke away from the main body and attacked the Tower of London and, to their delight, found the people who, they thought, were behind the poll taxes – the Archbishop of Canterbury, the King's treasurer and John Legge. They dragged them to Tower Hill and beheaded them.

Most of the peasants thought they had won the battle, when the King agreed to their demands and started to go home, but Watt Tyler and a group of rebels stayed behind and demanded to see the King again. The monarch agreed and met them in Mile End. It is said that the mayor of London thought that Tyler had insulted the King, by refusing to dismount and spitting on the ground. In anger he whipped out his sword and struck Watt Tyler on the neck. Mortally wounded, Tyler fell to the ground. Then, one of the King's squires administered the *coup de grace*. The mob became confused and most did not realise what had happened. In an instant, the young King realised how dangerous the situation was and, spurring his horse, rode into the middle of the mob. He is believed to have shouted, 'I am your King! I will be your leader! Follow me. All your demands will be met.' The peasants took him at his word and went home.

The King went back on his word, claiming he had signed the charter under duress, and he immediately sent troops out to capture and kill the rebels. The King took his court to Writtle and from there sent out proclamations to all the country, telling the population that the rebellion was over and all rebels would be punished, and so for seven days Writtle was the seat of government.

During the rebellion, the rebels had murdered the chief justice and so the King appointed Sir Robert Tresilian, who set up his court in Chelmsford, intent on bringing the traitors to justice. Many rebels, thinking they had the King's word, thought they were safe and a band of them camped in Norsey Woods, Billericay. When they were approached by the King's soldiers they waved a copy of the King's charter at them, but the solders had their orders and put the rebels to the sword. All over the country the rebels were hunted down and executed, often without trial. Despite the slaughter, the rebellion did have a positive side as the poll tax was never raised again until Margaret Thatcher did so in the 1980s, and it was soon repealed after ordinary people took to the streets. The Peasants' Revolt also gave the serfs some measure of freedom. Workers' wages were no longer controlled by Government, and the landlords had a certain respect for the peasants, as they feared there might be another rebellion.

DID YOU KNOW THAT...?

It is said that the ghosts of Civil-War soldiers have been seen standing outside St Mary's church, Great Baddow, where the Essex men gathered in the Peasants' Revolt of 1381. I wonder why Civil War soldiers? Could it be that the people who saw the soldiers were mistaken and that they were the spirits of the rebels that were executed following the revolt? It is understood that there are tunnels under the church and an ethereal monk has been seen walking towards a door that could lead into the tunnels.

St Marys church, Great Baddow, the place where the Essex rebels rallied in 1381.

The quiet village of Great Baddow, around the turn of the twentieth century.

Lock Up Your Daughters

It is difficult to believe that during the eighteenth century Chelmsford was swamped with more military personnel than civilians. The troops were on their way to Harwich, to embark for France to fight in the Napoleonic Wars. It is calculated that at one time there were more troops in Chelmsford than civilians. Every available space was taken up by them, every inn, barn, stable and church hall.

Napoleon planned an invasion of England in 1803 and built a large armada to carry out his plans. He assembled his fleet and army of 100,000 at Boulogne and declared he would plant the Imperial Eagle on the Tower of London. The regular army of England at that time was only 50,000 and so the government had to take urgent action. They doubled the size of the regular army and reinforced it with volunteer regiments, which raised the total number of men under arms to 150,000.

The volunteers' duties were laid down by Prince Frederick, the Duke of York. He knew the regular army was outnumbered by Napoleon's and so decided that if Napoleon did invade the army would not be able to defeat him in an open battle, therefore he decided to carry out a guerilla campaign, similar to that proposed by Churchill in the Second World War. They were to operate in small groups and harass the French if they landed. They were never to engage them in a full battle and were to retire when pressed. The plan was for the King and Government to move to Chelmsford or Dartford, depending on where the French landed.

The Loyal Chelmsford Volunteers were raised by Rector John Morgan in 1798, aided by Thomas and George Gepp (ancestors of the well-known Chelmsford Solicitors). Luckily, the regiment never had to be put to the test, although Capt. Gepp was drafted into the regular army. The Loyal Roxwell Volunteers were also formed at the same time, to defend Chelmsford. With the help of the Royal Engineers, both volunteer regiments constructed earthworks and gun emplacements to defend the route to London. They built two forts on a ridge to the south of Moulsham, one on Galleywood Racecourse, which was to defend the Maldon Road and one more at Widford, on the Clacton Road.

Lady Mildmay was somewhat upset when she found the regiments building earthworks on her land. Under the terms of her aunt's will she was forced to live in the house for a certain time each year, but objected to being encroached upon by soldiers. She found it impossible to live in the house so she let the army have it for the duration of the Napoleonic War. Once the threat of invasion subsided the Chelmsford Volunteers were disbanded in 1809.

With so many troops in Chelmsford crime rose to alarming heights. When the offending soldiers were caught, they were subjected to the cat-o-nine-tails. The offender received as many as 100 lashes while tied to a gun-carriage wheel. If the man fainted during the punishment, they waited until he had recovered and then resumed. Prisoners' backs were often stripped to the bone and many died under the punishment.

After the old prison on the Moulsham side of the stone bridge was pulled down, a barracks was built there to accommodate the West Essex Regiment and the 44th East Regiment of Foot. In 1782 the government decided to link regiments with areas of Britain and the 44th Foot Regiment became the 44th East Essex Regiment, whereas the Pompadours, the 56th, became the West Essex Regiment. Both regiments had been involved with campaigns across the globe, from France, North America, Cuba, Gibraltar and the West Indies.

Above left: A soldier of the 44 East Essex Regiment in uniform of around the time of the Napoleonic Wars.

Above right: Barrack Square today.

The old St John's Hospital, which was once a workhouse and before that, an army barracks.

The recent war in Afghanistan is not the only war we have had with the tribes of that country. The *Essex Chronicle* reported in 1839 on the war involving the British and the East India Co. fighting the Afghans. On this occasion we won, but we were defeated in the second Anglo-AfghanWar, which ran from 1878 to 1880, and again in 1919, when the *Essex Chronicle* reported our defeat.

'The Defeat of Napoleon'

It is difficult to believe that the *Essex Chronicle* carried reports of America's War of 1812–15, the battle of Waterloo and every important event since 1764. Its first edition appeared on the streets twenty four years before The Times.

William Strupar took over a printing works in Chelmsford High Street, where Marks & Spencer now stands, which is marked with a blue plaque. At first he sold magazines, Bibles, stories, plays and anything to do with writing, such as pens, quills, writing paper, and travelling cases. William Strupar realized that Essex did not have its own paper and as an experiment set up the *Essex Chronicle* or the *Essex Weekly Advertiser*. Soon it became a roaring success, reporting on world events and specialising in snippets of information that would be of interest to an Essex man. It reported on the deaths of 3,000 people in Naples, killed by an infectious disease which swept the city. He increased his circulation of the paper by advertising.

The paper reported on the French Revolution and the American War of 1812. They featured Napoleon's first exile to Elba in 1814 and his subsequent escape on the sailing ship, the *Swift*, and his hundred days' rise in France. The paper was filled with Napoleon's final defeat at Waterloo on the 18 June 1815, which in those days was the equivalent of winning the First World War and later, the Second World War.

After 251 years the paper is still going from strength to strength despite email and modern ways of communicating. In 1963 it started printing in colour. Over the years it had a number of moves, but is now based in Westway, Chelmsford and, I am glad to say, is still going strong.

Left: First World War aircraft.

Right: The 1764 birthplace of the *Essex Chronicle*.

The Royal Flying Corps

Just outside Chelmsford is the First World War Airfield of Stow Maries. It was one of the four aerodromes in Essex during the First World War. Although it was recognised by the junior ranks that aircraft would be very valuable in the First World War, many of the senior officers did not think so. It was not until they realised that Germany and France were increasing the production of aircraft that they changed their minds. Apart from very few aircraft, the other problem Britain had was a shortage of pilots. In 1912 Britain had only eleven pilots in the army and eight in the navy, whereas France had in the region of 260. As early as 1912 Germany was drawing up plans to raze London to the ground. Their Zeppelins, Gothas and heavy bombers were well advanced by the time the war started in 1914. The first attack did not take place until the spring of 1915. The casualties from the bombing were 1,000 deaths, which is not a huge number when compared with the 11,600 that were killed in the first thirty days of the Blitz during the Second World War. After the first attacks in 1915, people rioted and demanded that the government must do something about it. Their response was to establish the Home Defence Squadrons, whose role was to protect London's approach from the east.

37 Squadron moved into Stow Maries in 1916 with BE 12s aircraft, which were flimsy and mainly made of wood and paper and were very unreliable. Their first commanding officer was nineteen-year-old Lt Claude Ridley M. M. In March 1916, seven Zeppelins crossed the Channel with orders to attack London. Instead, they dropped their bombs on East Anglia. 37 Squadron was scrambled and Capt. Ridley took on one of the Zeppelins and fired while it was caught in a search light. Anti-aircraft guns opened up and scored a direct hit. It burst into flames and came down in the sea just off Margate. Prior to being stationed at Stow Maries, Capt. Ridley had fought on the Western Front, and one of his special tasks was to fly spies into Germany.

He was wounded at the Front and sent back to England to recover. When he did, the authorities thought that if he went back to the Front and got shot down in enemy lines, the Germans would shoot him as a spy and so they decided to give him the command of Stow Maries.

Stow Maries were allocated their first planes, the BE 12, which had proved unsuitable in France as they were not manoeuverable enough and could not reach the height of the German Zeppelins. They learnt later to wait until the Zeppelins returned to their hangars in Belgium to shoot them down as they lost height to land. As the war progressed, Stow Maries gradually received the better aeroplanes. It was flight C, stationed at Goldhanger, that had their first kill by shooting down Zeppelin L48 over Theberton in Suffolk. At first interceptions were rare and most Zeppelins crashed because of bad weather or mechanical failure, but as the War went on and communications improved the Royal Flying Corps' killing rate improved. Zeppelins became very vulnerable, especially when the Royal Flying Corps started to use bullets that exploded as they hit their target, sending the Zeppelins down in a ball of flames. Because of the Royal Flying Corps' success against the Zeppelins, the Germans abandoned them and relied on their Gotha planes and giant bombers.

Ten personnel lost their lives at Stow Maries. Two were shot down by friendly fire: the ack-ack thought they were enemy planes as they were caught in the search lights. The other pilots lost their lives in flying accidents, many after only a few flying hours. Originally, Stow Maries had been farmland since the thirteenth century and when the war started in 1914 it was being tenanted by Harry Turner. Then in 1916, the government requisitioned part of the farm for the airfield. In 1919, a year after the war, the squadron was transferred to Biggin Hill and the land was handed back. In 2009 Steve Wilson and Russell Savory bought the airfield.

At the height of the war there were 219 personnel on camp. Only twelve of them were women, who were then divided into two groups: those that could only work within 16 miles of their home and those that could go anywhere.

The airfield is currently being restored by a group of volunteers and is well worth a visit, especially on one of their flying days.

DID YOU KNOW THAT...?

There is a school of thought that the first powered flight was not by the Wright Brothers but by a flight from Fambridge, which was encouraged by the *Daily Mail*. This is disputed.

DID YOU KNOW THAT...?

Douglas Bader, the famous legless fighter pilot, trained in an Avro50K, which was a First World War plane that did not cease production until 1934.

Three men wearing First World War Royal Flying Corps uniforms watching a fly-past.

German Naval Airship Service Zeppelin L.32 in flight over Germany.

Above left: A Zeppelin in full flight, which instilled fear into the British people in the First World War.

Above right: A lady dressed in the uniform of the Women's Royal Flying Corps.

DID YOU KNOW THAT...?

Zeppelins used the Thames as a marker and followed it up to London, flying across Essex and often dropping their bombs on the way back or on the way there, if they were attacked. They did drop bombs on Chelmsford a number of times aiming for Marconi's and Hoffman's. There were 108 raids over Britain during the war and in one raid on Marconi's Factory, which took place on the 17 August 1915, the bomb went through the roof of a house in Glebe Road, just missing the lodger, who was in bed. It finished up embedded in the sofa below. Luckily it did not explode.

Another bomb dropped on Springfield and nearly knocked the police station out and shook up the Bishop of Chelmsford.

The Second World War

During the Second World War Chelmsford was a target for German bombing because of Hoffman's, the ball bearing factory, and Marconi, the radio and radar manufacturers. On the 13 May, 1943, a raid took place on the two factories but the bombs missed the factories and instead fell on Springfield and Moulsham Street, killing over fifty people and making nearly 1,000 people homeless.

Then, during the night in December 1944, a rocket dropped in Henry Street, near Hoffmans, killing thirty-nine people and injuring 138. It also destroyed a number of private houses. There is a monument to those killed in the cemetery in Writtle Road.

I remember the V2 rockets well. They fell out of the sky without warning and I have never forgotten that fear. I remember as a ten-year-old going to school and fearing that at any moment I could be killed. They were a lot worse than the Doodlebugs for you could hear

Hoffman's factory.

them coming, and when their engine cut you had time to fall flat on the floor; if you heard the explosion you knew you were safe but if you did not, you were dead!

Like many places in Chelmsford, Woolworths in the High Street had its own ARP (Air Raid Precautions). Woolworths was hit by an incendiary bomb (these were filled with various types of inflammable material, such as napalm, phosphorus and thermite). It set fire to part of the store and the staff bravely set about fighting the blaze with handheld stirrup pumps, finally putting it out. They cordoned off the area and were ready to open up to the public by 9.00 a.m. Some customers are never satisfied and complained that they could still smell burning.

Two of the victims of the bombing were Edmond Roper and his wife, who were killed in the early hours of the morning at their home, No. 28 Upper Bridge Road, on 21 November, 1940. A single German bomber opened his bomb doors, intending to hit Hoffman's, but instead killed two old-age pensioners. They were both found under a pile of rubble that was once their house. Mrs Roper was brought out dead, but her husband survived a few more hours in hospital.

In those far-off war days, bomb aiming was very inaccurate, not as it is today, and on their way back from a raid on London, the Luftwaffe would drop any spare bombs on the countryside or cities like Chelmsford.

To counteract the bombing in this area forty permanent gun sites were established within Essex. The gun emplacements were made of concrete and would hold a mixture of artillery and rockets. Some of the guns, such as the Borfor gun, could pump out 120 rounds a moment into the night sky. Remains of some sites could be seen right up until 1990, but time has played its part and many of the sites have now been cleared and used for farming or have been built on. In 1942 there was a gun emplacement in Baddow, which was called C9 Great Baddow. At that time it was manned by a section of the 84 Regiment. It had four guns, capable of firing 3.7 shells.

Some of the sites were operated by women, especially the searchlight units, which lit up the night sky, picking out enemy planes so that the gunners could see what they were aiming

Marconi's factory.

at. Once in the beam of the searchlight, the planes very rarely escaped the powerful light which seemed to follow them no matter what they did. One tactic the Germans used to escape the glaring beam was to dive-bomb it. I remember as a child standing on the veranda with my grandfather, watching the bright light sweeping the sky and seeing enemy planes caught in the beam and hearing the guns blasting away.

Another well-recorded gun emplacement was in the recreation ground, Central Park, which fired deadly rockets. It was manned by the Essex Home Guard. The unit trained in Writtle and moved to Central Park in 1943. It had sixty-four twin rockets. The battery shot down many enemy planes. To assist in locating a target they had radar, which was in its infancy. It was operated by two men, later by women, and was situated in the cricket ground. Sadly no remains of the site exist.

Some of the buildings that have survived the passing of time are the pillboxes that scatter the countryside at strategic points. There is one in a field near West Hanningfield, which I believe has a preservation order on it. There are also well-documented ones on and around the River Crouch at Battlebridge. They are 14 feet by 15 feet and normally have a 250-yard tank ditch in front of them. These pillboxes were built to guard the roads that the Germans would have come down, had they invaded. Another deterrent for tanks were pyramid-shaped blocks of concrete, which were designed to impede tanks in the case of an invasion, and were placed on the route that the army thought the Germans would take. Sadly, there are very few left but a few can still be seen on Dunwich Beach in Suffolk.

Gun bunkers of the Second World War on the old A130.

Hylands House.

'Gentlemen, I think you have taken the wrong turning!'

After the Second World War it was not wise to go digging in the grounds of Hylands House because you never knew what you might dig up. In 1944 the SAS took over the house while the owner, Lady Christine Hanbury, and her son, still occupied certain rooms. The SAS, being the SAS, had acquired more weapons than they had on record, and so when the time came for them to move out they had to get rid of the surplus. They buried them in the flower beds and for years afterwards they were being dug up by the gardeners.

During one night Lady Hanbury came out of her rooms to investigate the noise and to her horror found the staircase blocked by a Land Rover. One of the SAS men had driven it up the staircase. She is reported to have looked at the vehicle, glared at the driver and said, 'Gentlemen, I believe you have taken the wrong turning!' They got the Land Rover up but had to dismantle it to get it down.

The house played its role in a number of wars. Between 1803 and 1813, when Napoleon was threatening to invade England, it threw the country into a panic. The government thought that he might land his army at Harwich and then march on London. Troops were rushed to Chelmsford to prevent his advance. Gun emplacements and earthworks were thrown up round the town, including the grounds of Hylands House. Luckily, they were never put to the test.

During the First World War the house was requisitioned for a hospital and had over 100 beds. Sir Daniel Gooch, the owner, who bought Hylands in 1907, helped the war effort by ensuring the hospital had the most up-to-date equipment to treat its patients, while his wife supervised the nurses. The army used the vast grounds for training purposes and parades. A great parade was held in October 1914 when George V took the salute as 1,500 soldiers marched past.

During the Second World War a prisoner of war camp was set up in the grounds. The new owner of the house, Lady Christine Hanbury, who was a widow, allowed the Red Cross to set up a hospital there. When Lady Hanbury died in 1962, the house started to deteriorate and finally the council took it over. When their gardeners started cultivating the grounds they found that the SAS had planted some unusual crops!

DID YOU KNOW THAT...?

It is reported that Hylands House is haunted by a man wearing a long Victorian coat and top hat, who frequents the first floor of the house. There is also a young girl in the drawing room, who it is said appears when the piano is played.

On 5 June 1648, during the English Civil War, Essex's County Parliamentary Committee were meeting in Chelmsford when they were taken prisoner by a band of Royalists and dragged to Colchester. They were incarcerated during the siege of the town from 12 June to 28 August 1648. The Royalists made a number of attempts to break out from the city under the leadership of Sir Charles Lucas, but he was finally caught and executed. The Parliamentarians were lead by Sir Thomas Fairfax.

The Victoria Cross was first awarded in 1856 by Queen Victoria, following the Crimean War (1853–56) and was made from Russian guns captured at the Siege of Sevastopol. One of the types of cannon can be seen in the grounds of Chelmsford Museum. So far 1,356 Victoria Crosses have been awarded since its introduction. Twenty-three VCs were awarded during the Zulu War. The officer in command was Lord Chelmsford.

The captured Russian cannon from the Battle of Sevastopol, now in the grounds of Chelmsford Museum.

Saracen's Head Hotel during the Second World War.

Private Columbine was only twenty-four when he was killed on 22 March 1918, eight months before the war ended. He took charge of a machine gun and held back hundreds of Germans as they tried to advance. Sadly, in the end, he was killed by a bomb. During the Second World War the Saracen's Head was used by the American forces as a club similar to our NAAFI. A third of Chelmsford's Athletics Club were killed during the Second World War.

Secrets of Chelmsford's Public Houses

The Black Boy Inn

Probably one of the oldest pubs in Chelmsford was the Black Boy Inn, which, as far as one can tell, goes back to the sixteenth century when it was called The Crown Inn. Today Next (the clothes shop) stands in its place at the junction of the High Street and Springfield Road. It was a staging post on the way from Harwich, Colchester and London. When the Mildmay family and other landowners sold some of their land to the Eastern Counties Railway it spelt the death knell for this and other staging posts. Progress was slow and it took another fifty years before this much slower and more uncomfortable form of transport gave way to the open, smoky steam trains.

At one time The Black Boy was completely refurbished and was salubrious enough to have George IV stay. Its crowning glory was its large ballroom and it had stables for fifty horses. The Duke of Wellington, who won Waterloo, stayed in the inn. Charles Dickens was not impressed with Chelmsford when he stayed in The Black Boy while covering the election in Chelmsford for the *Morning Chronicle*. He is reported to have said 'Chelmsford is the dullest place in England and the only thing to look at are the two enormous prisons which are large enough to hold the whole population of Chelmsford.' It was pouring with rain at the time and no town looks its best in the rain.

Many meetings were held within its rooms, including the first meeting of the Board of Guardians of the Poor Law, where it was agreed that five more parishes would be added to the list. In 1777, the Chelmsford Tradesmen's Club met in The Black Boy but later moved to the Saracen's Head. The club was established to enable the commercial community to meet up, carry out business and auctions, including selling the Rising Sun Public House in Billericay on the 29 January 1830. Sadly the Black Boy Inn was demolished in 1857.

The Saracen's Head Inn

The Saracen's Head dates back to 1539 and was a coaching station like The Black Boy, serving travellers on the road from Harwich to London. It hired out post chaises which were complete with post boys who were ready and willing to take travellers on the next leg of their journey. Both inns had their own livery, the Saracen's Head being blue.

Records show that the inn was bought in 1718 by Thomas Nicholls for £650, which was an enormous price in those days. He must have been a very rich man to be able to pay back the mortgage, but when he started to carry out extensive alterations he ran out of money and had to sell the property to William Taylor.

In 1768 the Beefsteak Club was formed and met in one of the cellars once a month to coincide, as near as possible, with the date of the new moon. Each year the inn held

A drawing of the Black Boy Inn around 1800.

The site of the Black Boy Inn today.

a Flower Banquet. The inn was famous for its grand balls, which all the local nobility attended. A few years later, after 1791, business started to fail due to the opening of a rival venue – Shire Hall. Despite other inns in the area, Anthony Trollope (1815–82) chose to stay in the Saracen's Head while carrying out his job as inspector general for the Post Office. While he was in the Saracens' Head he wrote his weekly chapter of the Barchester Towers, no doubt while sipping a glass of wine. On a table opposite, he overheard two clergymen discussing the merits of his latest episode. One remarked, 'Confound that Mrs Proudie, I wish she was dead!'

Trollope shouted over his shoulder, 'Gentlemen, she dies next week.'

DID YOU KNOW THAT...?

During the Second World War the Saracen's Head was the headquarters of the equivalent to the British NAAFI. Scattered around Essex, Norfolk and Suffolk were many American airfields and the Saracen was where they could go to relax, read an American paper and eat what they would eat at home.

The ghostly Angel public house.

The Haunted Room.

The Angel

The Angel dates back to the fifteenth century and was originally a manor house that was converted into an inn in approximately 1702. It is said that the public house is haunted and there have been a number of reports of happenings. The public house has been investigated on a number of occasions. I spoke to Becky, a waitress who has worked at the Angel for nearly ten years, and she told me that she had seen a ghostly figure of a man in flowing robes on the stairs. She said that the man has been seen many times but that he prefers women and rarely shows himself to men. She also said that a number of people have seen the ghostly figure of a woman by the bar. A paranormal meeting was held at the public house and members of the group claim they experienced unexplained happenings while using an Ouija board. The séance was held downstairs in a small room where one member of the group claimed that he was unable to free himself from a negative energy until he was helped by other members of the group. During the four-hour investigation one of the group managed to capture a number of unexplained images of spirits that would not leave the building.

To celebrate Queen Victoria's Golden Jubilee in 1898, sixty notable people of Chelmsford sat down to a meal. It is also said that years ago, one of the back rooms was used as a brothel. It puts a different slant on going out for a quick one!

The *Spotted Dog*, a painting by Alfred Bamford. (Courtesy of Chelmsford Museum)

The Spotted Dog

If you are in the shopping centre and find boxes being thrown around and there is no explanation for it, put it down to 'The Box Monster.' The Spotted Dog Inn stood where the centre is now, at No. 24 Tindal Street, until it was demolished during the 1970s to make way for the new development. The Spotted Dog was many centuries old but in 1804 a Hanoverian regiment was passing through Chelmsford on their way to Harwich and France. Every available billet had been taken up; every inn, church hall and all that was left was the stables at the Spotted Dog. Thirteen of the regiment were housed in these for the night. The stables had a latch on the outside of the door that had to be opened by pushing something through the keyhole. During the night, it is thought that one of the soldiers must have emptied his pipe ash onto the straw, setting the building alight. Being dark and trapped in an unfamiliar building, as it got hotter, with the smoke filling the air they panicked trying to find a way out. They did not know how to operate the English lock. They shouted out for help in German but nobody understood until it was too late and flames were seen pouring out of the stables. When the fire was out thirteen charred bodies were found, and it is thought that 'The Box Monster' might be the soldier who accidentally started the fire and now kicks the boxes about in anger, because he now realises that his comrades' deaths were his fault.

The White Horse Inn on the left of the main street today.

The White Horse Inn

My wife and I have often had an excellent meal in The White Horse Inn in Great Baddow and because of its age (1600) it has an atmosphere. I have always suspected there was a ghost story connected with the building and when I was carrying out research for the book I was not disappointed.

Thomas Kidderminster owned a number of properties in Ely and decided to sell up and move to London. He sent his wife on ahead and said he still had business to attend to and he would join her later. He raised quite a lot of money from his sales and, with the cash in his purse, he set off to join his wife but he never arrived. His wife Anne was a very strong-minded woman and was determined to discover what had happened to her husband. Having just had a baby, she was certain he had not left her. She followed every lead but to no avail. For years she looked for him. Then, one day she saw a newspaper article which related how the owner of The White House Inn in Great Baddow had found a body while building a wall round the property. Anne was certain it was her husband's body as it was calculated that the man had been dead for ten years, which was around the time her husband disappeared. She set out to investigate.

On her way to the inn she passed through Romford and by coincidence met the maid, Mary, who had worked at The White Horse ten years before. She told Anne that the previous landlord, Mr Sewell, had been a bad man and should be hanged along with Moses Drayne, who worked with the horses at the inn. The former owner of the inn had died of the plague but his wife was still alive and so Mary questioned Mrs Sewell and found her answers were so vague that she was sure it was her husband's body. Anne stayed at The White Horse and was terrified when she heard noises in the room her husband had slept in. She claims she saw the latch of her door move in the night and the whole room shook with noise. She told the landlord what had happened the next morning and he said he was not surprised, as there had been a lot of unexplained things happening since he took over.

Still not having sufficient evidence to go to the police, Anne decided to question Mr Drayne, who had worked at the inn. She found him in a pub and asked him to describe the man who had stayed at The White Horse ten years before and was not surprised when his description matched that of her husband. Before Anne could gather any more evidence Mrs Sewell died, but the authorities issued a warrant for the arrest of Mr Drayne and Mary, the maid servant. Mary ran away but was soon caught and decided to confess. She said that she had gone into the front room just as Mr Kidderminster was handing over a bag of money to Mr Sewell for safekeeping and heard Mr Kidderminster tell Mr Sewell 'there is over £60 in the bag. Look after it'.

That night Mr Sewell instructed Mary to change her room and sleep at the far end of the inn, and she was surprised when she heard the key turn in the lock to her door. During the night she was woken by the sound of something being dragged across the floor of the landing. The following morning Mary saw the Sewell family sitting round the breakfast table, but they all looked tired out, as if they had not slept. She asked 'Where is Mr Kidderminster?' and was told he had left early.

Mary said she suspected foul play and to satisfy her curiosity, crept into the room that Mr Kidderminster had stayed in. She carefully opened a chest that was in the corner and found, to her surprise, Mr Kidderminster's clothes and his, now empty, money bag. Terrified, she ran downstairs and confronted Mrs Sewell, who attacked her. Then Mr Sewell came in to find out what the noise was. When he found out he offered Mary £20 to keep quiet. Reluctantly, Mary accepted the bribe. After her confession she was imprisoned. Both Mr Sewell and Mrs Sewell were already dead but Moses Drayne stood trial and was found guilty. He was hanged for his part in the murder. People who stay at the White Horse have said they have seen a ghost, but whose?

The Tulip as it is today.

Tulip

One of the most interesting public houses in Church Road is the Tulip public house. It is claimed that it is the only public house in England with the name Tulip. It was originally a farmhouse, owned by a Mr Drake. He ran the pub as a sideline to his day job, which was farming. No doubt he diversified because at the beginning of the nineteenth century farmers were having a hard time competing with the cheap imports of wheat and grain from America and Canada. In 1891, in places like Wickford and Basildon farmers were selling their land to the London Land Co., who divided up the land into plots and sold them to Londoners for as little as £10. Special trains were run to the stations where they were met by carts which took them off to the farms where the buyers were fed for 2/6 and plied with drink, encouraging the city dwellers to buy the plots. Some of the plot-landers would come down at weekends, loaded with material to build shacks. Some people put old buses on their plot or, in one case, the cabin of a boat. Some of them eventually lived in them, especially during the Second World War when some Londoners came down to escape the bombing. Following the war, the Government brought in the New Towns Act of 1946, which saw Basildon Development Corporation compulsorily purchasing these plots and build the new town of Basildon. (See my books on *Wickford Memories*, *Basildon Memories* and *Basildon Then and Now*).

The Riverside Inn.

The Riverside Inn (Formerly Springfield Mill)

One of the most picturesque public houses in Chelmsford is the seventeenth-century Riverside Inn. Like most of the old inns, it holds its secrets of murders, ghosts, intrigues and plots. In 1844 Chelmsford was rocked by the scandal of a baby being murdered by its mother and thrown in the river near The Riverside Inn (formerly Springfield Mill).

The mother was twenty-eight-year-old Elizabeth Belsham, who had a relationship, or was married to, Stephen Dean. She left the matrimonial home, no doubt after an argument with her partner over who was the father of the baby she was having. It was thought that he had thrown her out. She went to live with her mother while she had the baby. While she was there they received the sad news that her brother had died. Despite this tragedy she arranged for her son to be named Stephen James after him, and to be baptised at St Leonard's church, Southminster. When her son was only nineteen days old, Elizabeth decided to leave her mother's house in order to find a wet nurse for her son and to join her husband in their house in Baddow Road. She boarded a mail cart on its way to Chelmsford and expected to find her husband in the Beehive public house.

The mail cart stopped at an inn in Runsell Green and at her trial the landlady of the inn said she saw Elizabeth feed her son with two biscuits, despite the fact that he was less than a month old. She went on to say that she did not see Elizabeth take any refreshment herself. After a while Elizabeth continued her journey to The Beehive public house to find her husband, but when she arrived she was told he was not there. Carrying her son in her arms, she set off into the night to find him. Court witnesses said later that they saw her in The King's Head drying herself by the fire, but there was no sign of the baby. One witness swore she saw fresh gravel on Elizabeth's boots. Elizabeth stayed at the inn for the night and next morning wrote a brief note to her husband, telling him their son was dead. The husband did not seem particularly upset when he read the note because he was convinced that the baby was not his. Elizabeth changed her mind about seeing her husband and set off to her friend's house in Writtle.

Oliver Turner was walking to work, along the River Chelmer when he noticed a child's body in the river, caught up against one of the bridge's supports, near Springfield Mill (now The Riverside Inn). Panicking, he rushed into the inn and yelled for help. Mr Joseph rose to his feet and agreed to help Oliver. Outside, they both waded into the river and retrieved the body. They called the police, who started to investigate and it soon lead to Elizabeth's arrest. An inquest was held, at which Doctor Bird, who carried out the autopsy, concluded that the baby had been drowned, but added that after close examination he could find no other injuries. The coroner's jury gave a verdict of murder and Elizabeth was charged with her son's death.

A great crowd gathered outside Shire Hall in July 1844 to hear the trial. The judge and court officials had to push their way through the throng to get to the court. In the dock, Elizabeth was asked, 'Do you plead guilty or not guilty?'
A hush fell over the court as they waited for her reply and in a whisper she replied 'Not guilty Sir.'

She was defended by one of the most brilliant lawyers of his day, who knew how to play to the crowd and gain their sympathy. He asked what husband would turn his wife out into the streets just as she was about to give birth? The lawyer also brought out the fact that she had not eaten that day and this made her so dizzy that she slipped in the mud and to her horror, dropped her son in the river. He put up such a good argument that the jury found her not guilty.

The Endeavour

The Endeavour started off as a blacksmiths in the 1800s, but unfortunately the smithy was not making enough money to live on and so he opened up as a public house and ran both businesses side by side. Business must have been slack because the landlord was asked, and agreed, to house prisoners overnight while they were being transported or were being taken to be hanged on a green near the public house. It is not known whether they were chained to their beds or whether the landlord had a special room to lock them in.

The Public House was named after Captain Cook's ship and has kept the name ever since. It has not been possible to ascertain the connection with Captain Cook, nor whether or not he stayed there.

The Golden Fleece

The Golden Fleece public house was first established in 1654 and rebuilt in 1932. Chelmsford was once a wool-trading area, along with the West Country and the West Riding of Yorkshire. Wool was the backbone of England's economy, and during Henry VIII's reign the dead had to be buried in a woollen shroud, or the relations were fined. On Sundays it was required that people attend church and wear a woollen hat or be fined. During William III's reign (1650–1702) The Wool Act of 1699 forbade imports of wool or woollen products from Ireland and America.

The Woolsack or Woolpack and The Golden Fleece were stopping places for wool traders on their way to Maldon, to have their wool exported.

Gray & Sons

You cannot have public houses unless you have brewers, and one of the oldest in the district is Gray & Sons, who started brewing in 1828 behind the Black Boy Inn in Springfield Road. It has been suggested that originally both enterprises combined to carry out brewing. Gray's business grew and it became necessary to expand. In 1870 they found suitable premises in Maldon and traded there until 1954, when they returned to Chelmsford, but this time to Rignals Lane, Springfield. In 1974 they were taken over by Greene King, a well-known and established company that had been brewing in Bury St Edmunds since 1799.

The original Gray's buildings are still standing two centuries later and appear to have remained the same as in 1829. The buildings have been taken over by a restaurant and various other enterprises.

The Endeavour public house.

The Golden Fleece.

e Red Cow Temperance Hotel, Broomfield Road c.1900.

Above left: Gray & Sons Brewery, today a restaurant.

Above right: The Red Cow Temperance Hotel, Broomfield Road, *c.* 1900s. (Copyright Chelmsford Museum)

The Three Compasses.

The Three Compasses

One of the most picturesque public houses in the area that is said to be haunted is The Three Compasses, which is just outside Chelmsford in the village of West Hanningfield. It has served good ale and food continuously since the seventeenth century and the current landlady, Rosemary Cotton, has a noticeboard in the saloon displaying the names of all the licensees back to when the first pint was poured. It is not surprising that a public house dating back that far should have ghosts: there must have been many a plot hatched in times gone past. Rosemary has been the landlady for over thirty years and before that she and her husband ran it until he sadly died. Rosemary and her son John have both experienced strange happenings. Both have felt something brush past them and felt a presence.

The Red Cow Temperance Hotel, Around 1900

During the nineteenth century temperance groups were established to prevent drunkenness. Organizations like the churches, the Quakers and many others tried to encourage people to take the pledge not to drink. They provided alternatives to going down the pub by having musical entertainment, cycling, walking, organised games and holidays. They established eating houses and even hotels to encourage people to stop drinking. The first Temperance Hotel was established in Preston and the movement soon spread all over the country.

Paper Mill Lock during the nineteenth century.

Chelmsford Transport Through the Ages

The Chelmer and Blackwater Canal

It is little realised that the canal, which was completed in 1797, is the shallowest in England, being only 2 feet deep in parts. It was one of the main arteries into the city, but because of the many objections to the scheme it nearly wasn't built. For over a hundred years those providing services by road, like hauliers and packhorse businesses, thought a canal would ruin them and objected to one being created. When the plans were published, Maldon Council came out strongly against them because the planned line of the canal did not pass through their town.

John Rennie was appointed as chief engineer, but he chose not to visit the site often and left the supervision to Richard Coates, who lived on the site. The canal runs for 13 miles, from Springfield Basin, Chelmsford, to the sea lock at Heybridge Basin, and was completed in an amazing time of four years. Having completed the job, Richard Coates decided to set up a barge company himself. One of the quays was named after him and he is buried in St. Morg's Saints' church, Springfield.

The original canal company ran the canal until 2003, when it was taken over by the Essex Waterways Association. From Heybridge Lock to the town there are thirteen locks. The original barges were 16 feet long and were pulled by horses until 1960, when the boats were motorised. They carried practically anything: bricks, stone, wood, grain and, once the gasworks were built in 1819, coal.

The birth of the railway in 1842 was the beginning of the end for the canal, but after the Second World War it was given a new lease of life when the sea lock at Heybridge was opened. This enabled European ships to enter and load timber onto barges, and the trade lasted right up until 1972 when the last barge unloaded the wood it was carrying into Brown's yard.

One of the pleasures today is to cruise along the canal in one of their boats or in a canoe from Paper Mill Lock, and round off the day with a cream tea.

Bus Services

A horse-drawn service was set up in 1730 and travelled from Chelmsford to London. But one had to get up early to catch it, as the bus left Chelmsford at 3.00 a.m. When the railway was introduced to Chelmsford in 1885 the coach could not compete, and so the firm went out of business. Steam buses arrived on Chelmsford's earth roads in 1903. The steam buses used oil as fuel as their boilers were designed differently to the traction engine.

The steam buses were manufactured by Thomas Clarkson, who was born in 1864. The top decks of the buses were open to the elements. The drivers must have found it very

Paper Mill Lock today.

Bus station during the 1950s. (Copyright Essex Record Office)

The bus station today. (Copyright Essex Record Office)

The rail station during the early 1900s.

uncomfortable as the buses had no windscreens. In 1912 the Great Eastern bus service took over from the National Steam Co. and operated out of Chelmsford.

A new bus station was opened in 1931 but did not escape damage during the Second World War. On the 14 May 1943 a bomb was dropped on it, destroying thirteen buses. The fire spread to surrounding houses and it took over two hours to put out. In no time at all it was repaired and lasted until recent years when it was replaced by the more modern one. Buses today are run by First Group, who have 381 buses on the road.

Railways

Around 1840 the Mildmay Family saw the potential of the railways and gathered some businessmen together to sell off a corridor of land to the Eastern Counties Railway Co., which, they knew, would dictate the route that the railway would take into Chelmsford. Before the railway could be built it was necessary to construct eighteen viaducts. The largest of these is in Central Park. It is 45 feet high and 18 feet wide. Another spans the river, while the last one was built so that it finished at the station.

The railway arrived in Chelmsford in 1842, but the three-storey station was not completed until 1885.

The railways became very popular despite the carriages being open to the elements and the passengers arriving at their destinations covered in soot. Soon they overtook the other means of transport that had served the population for centuries, like the picturesque horse-drawn coaches. The demise of this means of transport brought about the gradual death of the staging inns, as trains travelled a lot faster than the stagecoaches. Travellers could reach their destinations in a day and did not have to break their journey and stay overnight.

It was not long before the rail network had spread over most of the country and Royal Mail soon took advantage of this new form of transport, which meant that letters could be delivered overnight instead of days. Soon, the railways were running excursions to the seaside and at a price the ordinary working man could afford. The railways changed the country and in Chelmsford a number of business people formed the Chelmsford Co., whose aim was to develop the town. They proposed a new bridge over the river and a new London Road, with mansions leading into the town, to create a good impression on visitors. As a result the Fenton Iron Bridge was built, connecting New London Road to the town. The construction was completed in 1840, but sadly all their work was swept away in the floods of 1888.

A ghost is thought to reside in a storeroom at the railway station and was experienced by a plumber, who had a stack of chairs and tables fall behind him when they were perfectly balanced when he went in.

Hovercraft

Christopher Cockerell, as we all know, invented the hovercraft. He was born in Cambridge in 1910 and was also educated there. When he was twenty-five he started work at Marconi

The Railway Viaduct during the present time but built in the 1800s.

and helped to develop the radar systems, which he considered being one of his greatest achievements. The invention helped to win the Second World War.

While he was at Marconi he had the idea for the hovercraft, and to test out his theories he made a working model out of an old, used hair-dryer and two cans. When he was satisfied it would work, he tried to obtain finance to develop his idea but nobody would lend him the necessary funds and so he financed it himself. For four long years he worked on the project and then, finally, in 1955, his prototype craft was ready and he tested it by crossing the English Channel. Soon his invention was wanted all over the world.

He was knighted in 1969 for his services to industry. In 1999, at the age of eighty-eight, he died at his Hampshire home. A memorial was erected in his honour.

Some Interesting Chelmsford Citizens

Thomas Watts, Burnt to Death

During the reign of Bloody Mary (1553–58), 283 Protestants were burnt at the stake for their religion. Thomas Watts was a draper and lived in Billericay. He was a Protestant and was taken before the bishop on a number of occasions because he would not attend the Roman Catholic Church. The bishop tried to persuade him to change his religion but he refused. Finally on 5 April 1555 he, Thomas Hakes, Mary Askew and six others were brought before the commissioners to be examined by Lord Rich as to why they did not believe in the 'true religion'. They were all found guilty of not believing in the 'true religion' and were condemned to be burnt at the stake.

As he stood there in chains, waiting for the fire to be lit he turned and kissed the stake and shouted out for Lord Rich to repent. Then as the flames licked around him and his flesh started to singe, he roared out 'God will avenge my death!' Some reports say he was burnt near Shire Hall; others say it was by the side of the Stone Bridge. Whichever site, he was a brave man. The other eight suffered the same fate but in different locations, ranging from Braintree to Brentwood.

Sir Evelyn Wood

There are few people in Chelmsford who have fought in so many wars, risen through the ranks and been decorated with the VC as Sir Evelyn Wood. This courageous man was born in Cressing, Essex, in 1838. He was the youngest of five children and was well connected, which in those days would have helped his career. One of his uncles was an admiral and another was a captain in the Royal Navy. No doubt between the two uncles they procured their nephew a position of midshipman in the navy at sixteen years old. Within a short time he was manning the guns on a ridge opposite Sevastopol, in the Crimean War. During the battle he was wounded and for his bravery was recommended for the VC by his senior officer, but he was not awarded it.

Lord Raglan, of the Charge of the Light Brigade, gave Sir Evelyn a recommendation for the army and so he left the navy and joined them instead. In those days if you wanted to be an officer you could purchase your rank. He bought a commission with the 13th Light Dragoons and was soon back in the Crimea, but, as with many of the troops in that war, he was taken ill and repatriated.

He made a speedy recovery and was anxious to get back to the Front. His family helped him to purchase the rank of Lieutenant in the 7th Lancers and he was posted to India to help quell the Indian Mutiny (1857–58). While he was there he saw a band of rebels

Picture of Sir Evelyn Wood.

dragging an Indian shopkeeper into the jungle with the intention of hanging him. Almost single-handedly he charged the rebels, who made a stand and fought back, but young Lt Wood soon put them to flight.

In 1860, while still in India, he caught a fever, which was so bad that he had to be shipped back to England for treatment. It took him a year to recover and when he did so he purchased the rank of captain for £1,000 and paid a further £1,500 to his departing predecessor. With his eye on promotion he applied, and was accepted for further training at the Staff College in Camberley, which was set up in 1802. Having passed out of college, he looked for a staff position. He obtained one in Dublin as aide-de-camp, but he was soon back in England with poor health. It was not long before he was made a full major, at the cost of another £2,000. Shortly after that, the services stopped the system of buying promotion. He was put in command of part of the army training camp in Aldershot.

No doubt tired of having an office job, in 1874 he applied to serve in the Anglo-Ashanti War and fought in the battles of Amoaful and Esaman. He was wounded again, but managed to raise a regiment of Africans, although secretly he had a very poor opinion of their fighting abilities. He was very radical for his day and encouraged his officers to refrain from beating their African troops under their command.

Back in England, he was made a Companion of the Order of the Bath and was appointed superintendent of a garrison at Aldershot. In 1878, Sir Evelyn was again in the thick of the fighting with the 90th Light Infantry in Africa, and fought in the Battle of Tutu Bush. In 1879, he fought in the Zulu War and commanded one of the five columns who crossed the Zulu frontier. After Britain's defeat at Isandlwana he retreated to Kambula where the army set up defensive positions. He had his horse shot from under him at Hobane and finally helped to defeat the Zulus at Ulundi on 3 July 1879. Lord Chelmsford had learned his lesson after the Battle of Isandlwana, and this time, instead of the thin red line advancing, he formed his troops into a hollow square with the cavalry in a supporting role on the outside.

Sir Evelyn returned to Britain and was promoted to a staff officer, taking command of Chatham Garrison. But with his knowledge and experience in Africa, it made sense to send him back to Africa to fight in the Boer War in 1881. After the death of the governor of Natal, Staff Officer Wood was appointed to succeed him. Against his better judgment he was ordered to make peace with the Boers and agree a truce. As a result of the treaty, and having made a good impression on Queen Victoria and the prime minister, he was promoted to Major General and stayed in Natal for a while. In 1882 he returned to England and took up command of Chatham Garrison, but for only a short time as in the same year he was sent to Egypt.

In Egypt he was given command of the Egyptian Army, which he reorganised. The Urabi revolt broke out in Egypt and Wood was again in the thick of it. He had Kitchener under his command. When a column was sent out to relieve General Gordon at Khartoum, he made sure there was good communication and was in the battle of Ginnis.

Back in England he realised that the army marches on its stomach and he had army cooks trained. He carried out other reforms and before anyone else, saw the potential of bicycles and night marches.

He retired in 1904, lived in Essex and was appointed Constable of the Tower of London. He was given many others honours, including Colonel of the 5th Battalion the Essex Regiment, and was made the first freeman of Chelmsford. He died in 1919 and is buried at the Military Cemetery in Aldershot.

Above left: Cetshwayo, King of the Zulus, *c.* 1875

Above right: Lord Chelmsford.

DID YOU KNOW THAT...?

The battle of Ginnis, in which Wood took part, was the last battle in which the army wore red uniforms.

Frederic Thesiger 2nd Baron of Chelmsford

It is rare for two men to have similar careers and command troops in the same battles, but Gen. Frederic Thesiger and Sir Evelyn Wood did. Frederic was born on the 31 May 1827 and was one year younger than Sir Evelyn Wood. Thesiger's father was a lawyer who climbed the social ladder and eventually became Lord Chancellor. He was created Baron of Chelmsford. From an early age, Frederic was determined to join the army. At seventeen he applied to join the Guards, but was turned down. Not to be outdone, he bought a commission with the Rifle Brigade and served in Canada and then achieved one of his ambitions by purchasing a commission in the Guards.

Like Wood he served in the Crimean War, where he rose to be Deputy Assistant Quartermaster General. He saw action and was mentioned in dispatches and awarded a number of medals, including the Turkish and Sardinian Campaign Medals. He bought his promotion to Captain and then Lieutenant–Colonel in the 95th Derbyshire Foot Regiment, and towards the end of the Indian Mutiny was posted there. He was promoted in India to brevet colonel, which meant that he had the rank and responsibilities of a colonel but not the pay to go with it. In 1863 he served in Abyssinia, for which Queen Victoria awarded him the Companion of the Order of the Bath and made him aide-de-camp to her.

In 1869 he was off again to another part of the world, and this time it was the East Indies. After he returned home he was put in command of the army at Shorncliffe and then at Aldershot. In October 1878 his father died and he inherited his title, becoming the 2nd Baron Chelmsford. Bored with being stationed at home, and the fact that it was cheaper living abroad, he requested that he was posted to South Africa, where he helped to bring one hundred years of fighting between the settlers in Africa and the Xhosa tribe to an end. The tribe had swept across the border and laid to waste many European settlements.

A year later he was embroiled in the Zulu War. The war was engineered by Sir Bartle Frere, who broke the treaty between Cetshwayo, the Zulu King, and Britain. The British Army under his command crossed the border with 15,000 troops split into five. His intention was to attack the Zulus in their homeland. Wood commanded one of the five columns. The Zulus attacked the centre one at Isandlwana, the British Army were taken completely by surprise, paying the price of setting up camp without defences. The Zulus attacked, using their very successful tactics of the buffalo head with two horns, which encircled the British Army. The Zulu Army mainly fought with spears and cowhide shields but did have a few ancient Brown Bess rifles, while the British Army had the new Martini Henry rifles. Despite the British troops having superior weapons, they had great difficulty in opening their ammunition boxes. The number of soldiers slaughtered varies from 1,300 to 1,800, with only forty on horseback surviving. It was one of the British Army's greatest defeats by a native force. The column's commander, Durnford, was killed. As a result of the defeat the government immediately replaced Lord Chelmsford with Sir Garnet Wolseley, but before he could take over Chelmsford defeated the Zulus at the Battle of Ulundi. At the subsequent enquiry Chelmsford blamed Durnford for disobeying his orders and not setting up suitable defences. General Wolseley gave Chelmsford the credit of beating the Zulus at Ulundi. Chelmsford was awarded the GCB.

In 1882 Chelmsford was made a Lieutenant General and became Lieutenant of the Tower of London. He lived until 1905, when he suffered a seizure and died while enjoying a game of billiards in the United Service Club. One of his four sons became Viceroy of India.

Cuckoo's farm, Little Badow, where Thomas Hooker lived.

Father of Connecticut, America, Thomas Hooker

Thomas Hooker was born it is thought, in Marefield, Leicestershire, in the year 1586. He went to school at Market Bosworth and finished his education at Queen's College Cambridge, where he earned a Batchelor of Arts degree. After he finished his education he started preaching at Esher parish church and found that he had a flair for it. One of his parishioners was a Mrs Drake, who had a great influence on his thinking.

His preaching fame spread, and in 1625 he was invited to preach in St Mary's church, Chelmsford (now the Cathedral). At that time Chelmsford was noted for its riotous living and had a large number of inns and public houses. The population of Chelmsford flocked to hear him preach. Soon, he was made a curate and for three years he continued to preach and attract large congregations. It was not long before the Archbishop of Canterbury got to hear of him and he objected to Thomas's puritanical views, ordering him to stop preaching them. Thomas was forced to stop preaching and went to live in Cuckoo's Farm, Little Baddow. In view of the fact that he was a leader in the Puritan views, the Court of High Commissions summoned him to attend a hearing. He refused and fled to Holland, where they were more sympathetic to his views.

While in Holland he decided to emigrate to America and booked a passage on the *Griffin*. In Europe, puritans were being persecuted for their religion and many were emigrating to New England, like the Pilgrim Fathers in 1620.

In America, he settled in Newtown and became a pastor. He soon fell out with the leaders of the church because they would only allow people to vote who were members of their church. In 1636 Thomas Hooker and the Revd Stone decided to move out of the area and, with 100 followers, trekked to Hartford. Not long after, Hooker decided to take up American politics and was elected the representative for Hartford and Windsor. In 1638 Hooker and

Stone drew up a written constitution called the 'Fundamental Orders of Connecticut'. This document became the basis of America's democracy today.

Unfortunately for America, he became sick and died in 1647, at the age of sixty-one. His grave is unknown and there are no images of him, so nobody knows what the founder of American Democracy looks like.

Ronald Skirth

The First World War produced many heroes but it also produced men who fought but found they did not like to kill. Ronald Skirth was one such man.

He was born in Chelmsford on the 11 December 1897. In 1915, at the age of eighteen, he joined up and was sent to the Front in France. During the war he was involved in the battles of Messines and Passchendaele, where two of his friends were killed. Their deaths had a profound effect on him. Not long after, he came across the body of a German soldier of around his age, and was horrified when he thought that one of his shells might have killed him. After that, he was determined to give the enemy a warning by deliberately aiming the first shell so that it missed, giving the enemy time to take cover. He managed to disguise what he was doing because he was responsible for aiming the gun.

When he was demobbed he remained a Pacifist for the rest of his life, even advocating that we should not have gone to war with Germany in 1939. He became a teacher and when he retired, started to handwrite a book about his relationship with his wife. He then decided to write about his experiences in the First World War, describing his disillusionment with war and how he became a Pacifist. He gave the script to his daughter, who at first found it too upsetting to read. She finally read it and gave the script to the Imperial War Museum. They called his account 'The Reluctant Tommy' but it was not published until 2010, when it became a bestseller.

King Edward VI School that Joseph Strutt attended.

Joseph Strutt and the Root of the Olympics

The modern Olympic Games have their roots in Chelmsford, and were a result of a famous book entitled *The Sports and Pastimes of the People of England*, which was written by Joseph Strutt in 1801, a year before he died. Strutt's book had an influence on Dr William Brookes, who in 1850 started a village games in Much Wenlock. He wanted the games to improve the physique, morale and minds of the inhabitants of the village.

Baron Pierre de Coubertin heard about the games in the village and thought he should promote them worldwide, establishing the modern Olympic Games in 1896.

Joseph Strutt was born in 1749, in Springfield Mill. Unfortunately his father died soon after he was born, but despite this he managed to get into the famous King Edward VI School in Chelmsford, where a house is named after him. At the early age of fourteen he became an apprentice to a London engraver.

At the age of twenty-one he started to study at the Royal Academy and became one of their star pupils; he was one of the first students to win medals for his work. He decided he wanted to write and illustrate books so he spent months in the reading room of the British Museum researching material for his first book, *The Regal and Ecclesiastical Antiquities of England*. In the book he drew and engraved likenesses of kings as well as ancient items of interest.

He went on to write a number of other books that were well researched and of a similar vein, and had numerous illustrations of his in them. At the time, he was alternating between Chelmsford and London. When he was twenty-five he married Anne Blower, who lived in Bocking in Essex. He worked on thirteen engravings for an edition of *Pilgrims Progress*. He then decided to start writing fiction but unfortunately he died before it was finished. It was completed by no less a person than Sir Walter Scott, in 1802. I think this gives an indication of the writing standard of this citizen of Chelmsford, who has never received the recognition he deserved.

The Chelmsford Club, the house that James Fenton designed and lived in from 1846–57.

James Fenton, Architect

James Fenton was an architect and in 1830 he set up his practice in Chelmsford. He specialised in the design of workhouses and chapels. In 1839 he joined up with five like-minded people and formed a company which developed the New London Road that included a new iron bridge over the River Can. Unfortunately, during the floods in 1888 it was swept away.

He was given the post of surveyor to the Chelmsford Local Board of Health. Chelmsford City has a lot to thank him for, as he planned and implemented a water and sewage system. Prior to his work, Chelmsford was a very unhealthy place, with frequent outbreaks of cholera. He made such a good job of it that other boroughs sought his services and in 1857 he accepted a post with Croydon Health Board. It was fitting that when he died he was returned to Chelmsford and was buried in the Non-Conformist cemetery in New London Road.

Blackshirts in Chelmsford

On 18 May 1935 the corn exchange that once stood in Tindal Square was taken over by Sir Oswald Mosley's Blackshirts. He had been invited to speak in Chelmsford by the town's Fascist Association. As Mosley strutted onto the stage the audience rose, and with one accord gave the fascist salute. Looking at the black-shirted bully boys surrounding the audience, nobody dared to heckle Mosley as he ranted on for two hours, explaining the aims of the party and answering carefully worded questions.

Sir Oswald Mosley had fought in the First World War and after being commissioned in the 16th Queens Lancers he transferred to the Royal Flying Corps as an observer. Unfortunately his aeroplane crashed. After he was demobilized he became the Conservative member of parliament for Harrow (1918–24) and was also the youngest member. He fell out with the party's line over the use of the Black and Tans in Ireland and for a while became an Independent member of parliament. In 1926 he crossed the floor and became a Labour MP for Smethwick. Ramsay MacDonald made him the Chancellor of the Duchy of Lancaster, but he resigned when he disagreed with the Labour party's policies on unemployment. It was then he formed his new party entitled the British Union of Fascists, which was associated with Germany's Nazi party. When his wife died he married his mistress, Diana Guinness. The ceremony took place in Germany and one of their guests was Adolf Hitler.

In 1936 Mosley was determined to march through the Jewish area of the East End of London, which resulted in the Battle of Cable Street, where knives, razor blades and truncheons were used. The battle was finally stopped by the police but only after a lot of blood was spilt. During the Second World War he, his wife and son were interned in a house in Holloway Prison. They were released in November 1943.

The venue for Mosley's notorious meeting in Chelmsford was the historic corn exchange, which was designed by Frederic Chancellor and opened in 1857. It was used mainly, as the name implies, as a market where corn could be bought and sold, but unfortunately it was found to be unsuitable because the hall was poorly lit and merchants were unable to examine the corn for mould. The hall measured 100 feet by 45 feet, and although it was unsuitable for

The Corn Exchange, late nineteenth century.

The site of Cock & Bell public house in Writtle, now Bridge Road restaurant.

the purpose for which it was built, it was used for auctions, and entertainment. The building also contained a number of offices.

Peter Eckersley

It is generally thought that Marconi was the first to carry out broadcasting, with their transmission of Dame Nellie Melba, but that was just a one off. The first regular broadcasts were carried out by Peter Eckersley, from the Cock and Bell public house in Writtle. His transmissions went out every Tuesday at lunchtime. He had been in the RAF and worked as an engineer.

When Peter Eckersley was born in 1892, his father was working in Mexico as an engineer for the Grand Mexican Railway. Peter must have come from a very clever family as apart from his father being an engineer, his brother was a physicist. During the First World War Peter became a wireless engineer in the Royal Flying Corps. Following his demobilization he joined Marconi as a wireless engineer, and as a sideline set up the first licensed radio station in Writtle, giving regular weekly broadcasts, his first being excerpts from *Cyrano de Bergerac*. The actress Agnes Travers played Roxane and her brother Ben, Christian. Ben had also been in the Royal Flying Corps. Peter recited poetry and sang in his programmes. He gave a lecture on broadcasting to a great crowd of children in Folkestone at an annual conference and made the claim that broadcasting had started in Chelmsford, not America. In 1922 he applied for and was appointed chief engineer to the British Broadcasting Co. He held this post until 1927 when he was forced out by John Reith, who was a very religious man and objected to Peter having an affair with the programmer's wife Dorothy Clark, taking her to Germany on business. Dorothy had been separated from her husband for some time; the couple eventually married.

Dorothy was an admirer of Hitler and a member of the Imperial Fascist League. She counted William Joyce (better known as Lord Haw-Haw) as her friend. He was the traitor who broadcast from Germany during the Second World War and was finally hanged for treason. Peter Eckersley befriended Sir Oswald Mosley and was responsible for setting up in Germany the radio station from which Lord Haw-Haw broadcast. He helped to build many more broadcasting stations on the continent, whose programmers could be heard in Britain. He then started to introduce wired radio, rather like the cable television in Britain today, but the enterprise was stopped by the authorities.

It would appear that he still had Hitler's sympathies and attended some of his rallies before the war, but once the war started he commenced work in British intelligence. The couple split up and his wife stayed in Germany, working for German radio. After the war she and her son James were tried for helping the enemy. She was sentenced to a year in prison and her son was bound over for two years. Ironically, Peter and his wife died in the same year – 1971.

Mildmay

One of the most famous families in Chelmsford was the Mildmays, who, it is thought, came over with the Normans in 1066. For 500 years they have played a part in the history of Chelmsford. They bought the Friary in Moulsham following the Dissolution of the

A sketch of Thomas Mildmay.
(Copyright Chelmsford Museum)

Monasteries, and later purchased the Manor of Moulsham. In 1563 they expanded by buying up Chelmsford itself from Elizabeth I. The family bought Manor Hall, which was a large house with extensive grounds.

Thomas Mildmay had made his fortune overseeing the surrender of the monasteries under Henry VIII. He had been granted Moulsham and built a larger house for the family. In view of his father's large fortune and connections, Walter Mildmay had a good start in life, although he did not finish his degree course at Cambridge. He made up for this later by studying law.

When the Court of Augmentation was reconstituted in 1545, two years before Henry's death, Walter was made one of the surveyors to help control and administer the monastery which had been seized from the church. He was knighted for his efforts and after a number of promotions was given a commission to report on the King's finances and on the King's behalf sell the land they had taken. Under Queen Elizabeth I he set up Emmanuel College in Cambridge on the site that had been the Dominican monks' residence.

In 1536 there were 800 monasteries and over 10,000 people serving them in the form of monks, priests, nuns and bishops etc. By 1540 there were practically none. Walter Mildmay was the original governor of King Edward VI Grammar School in 1551. He died in 1589.

Walter Mildmay's brother Thomas was auditor to the Court of Augmentation. No doubt he kept an eye on his brother. Walter's eldest son Sir Anthony Mildmay inherited the estate of Apethorp and was an ambassador in Paris.

Women's Rights Movement

Anne Knight

It is little known that the roots of the suffragette movement started partially in Chelmsford by Anne Knight. She was born in 1786, near where the railway station is now. She had seven brothers and sisters and was the third child of William Knight, a grocer, and Priscilla. The whole family were Quakers and played a major part in the temperance and later the anti-slavery movements.

Anne helped to set up the women's branch of Chelmsford's Anti-Slavery Society. She travelled to Germany and France when she was thirty-eight and, with a working knowledge of both languages, was able to communicate with both communities. While she was on the continent she campaigned for the abolition of the slave trade and when the trading of slaves was outlawed in 1807 she could not see why the slave traders should be compensated and objected to the fact that the act did not ban keeping slaves. The Slavery Society was formed in 1823 and ten years later the Slavery Abolition Bill was passed so that the keeping of slaves was illegal. There were exemptions for the East India Company, Island of Ceylon and St Helena. It was another ten years before the law was changed and applied to them.

Anne not only campaigned for the abolition of slavery, she fought for women's rights and arranged meetings for both organisations. She also wrote and distributed pamphlets on both issues. She asked George Thompson (a well-known abolitionist) to speak in France but he declined and so, undaunted, she took on the tour herself.

Women did not have the same rights as men in 1840 and when The World Anti-Slavery Convention was held in London, women were excluded. This convinced Anne that there was a need to campaign for women's rights. It could have been no coincidence that this was the same year that she published statements and handbills. She also fixed labels to envelopes advocating women's rights and it is claimed that they were the first leaflets on women's suffrage.

She was furious when in 1850 the *Brighton Herald* suggested in an article that the fight for women's rights was less important than the class struggle. In protest, she wrote a letter to them. She assisted in setting up the first association for women's suffrage in Sheffield and they held their first meeting in 1851.

She was a woman of action and in 1849 got involved with the French Revolution. Nobody is sure whether Knightsville in Jamaica was named after her or her sister Maria. By 1850 she was sixty-four and moved to Waldersbach in France. She never married and died there at the age of seventy-six.

It is fitting that some of the student accommodation in Essex University is named after her and the Quaker Housing Association have named a hostel after her.

Grace Chappelow

Among the 200 women arrested in London in 1911 for protesting for women's rights was Grace Chappelow. She was an Essex Girl and was born in Hatfield Peverel. She was accused and convicted of breaking windows. In prison, like so many of the suffragettes, she went on hunger strike but unlike many of the suffragettes she was spared the indignity of being force-fed. She was a vegetarian and only drank goat's milk.

She met Mrs Konter (another active suffragette) who lived in Clacton and Grace moved in with her when her parents died. She had a dispute with a Conservative agent and was imprisoned when her dog bit him.

In 1912, Grace and some members of the Woman's Movement were brought before Bow Magistrates Court charged with breaking the windows of government buildings. Their solicitor pleaded that they had no previous convictions, that they were daughters of very respected men of Essex and that they were members of the Women's Social and Political Union in Clacton. The damage had not amounted to much and he asked if they could be fined instead of being given a prison sentence. The magistrates ignored the plea and sentenced them each to two months' imprisonment.

In 1897 Millicent Fawcett founded the National Union of Women's Suffrage Societies. Her sister Elizabeth was the first woman in England to qualify as a doctor, after a long struggle against prejudice. By 1905 it appeared that the press had lost interest in the campaign and some of the suffragettes decided to take direct action by cutting telephone wires and burning empty buildings. In 1903 Emily Pankhurst broke away from the National Union of Women's Suffrage and formed the Women's Social and Political Union. Her society became more militant and their membership grew out of all recognition, reaching over 2,000 at its peak. Women finally got the vote in 1918 but only for women over thirty. They did not get the full vote until ten years later in 1928.

The previous bridge to this one was the bridge where John Green prevented victims of the plague from crossing into Chelmsford.

Caring in Chelmsford

The Black Death

The Moulsham area of Chelmsford is thought to be the oldest part of the city, with ceramics of the Neolithic period (4,000 BC) having been found there. There is evidence of other occupations stretching back to Bronze, Iron and Roman times. The Romans constructed a bridge and fort on the southern side of the River Can. It is thought that Moulsham Street follows the Roman line south towards London. In AD 1,100 the Roman Bridge collapsed and another one was built. Moulsham was mentioned in the Domesday Book and at that time was owned by the Abbot of Westminster, while the rest of Chelmsford was owned by the Bishop of London.

The Moulsham area was hit by an outbreak of bubonic plague in 1349 when over thirty families were wiped out. Another infestation again occurred in the Moulsham area of the city in 1665. The area was very run down and the citizens were very poor and destitute, which were the perfect conditions to allow the disease to spread rapidly. The Black Death, as the plague came to be called, was caused by fleas from black rats. The symptoms were swelling of the glands in the armpits and groin, change of skin colour, bleeding, aching and decaying skin. Death normally occurred in four days.

John Spight was the first recorded victim. He was a map-maker who worked in Moulsham. The authorities in the Chelmsford area decided to try to keep the disease confined to the Moulsham side of the city and appointed John Green to look after the infected and to prevent anyone from Moulsham crossing the bridge into Chelmsford. Dwellings that had housed anybody living with the plague had a large red cross painted on the door, and when the person died the door was nailed up. For over a month John Green prevented the disease spreading to the other side of the bridge, but finally it broke out in the rest of the city causing around 20 per cent of the population to die. Each night the dreaded cry would go out: 'Bring out your dead.' People would pile the dead on carts and the bodies would be buried in a field nearby.

In the 1665 outbreak it is believed that coffins used to bury the victims of the Black Death were stored in an outhouse adjacent to The Rising Sun public house.

Destitute in the 1800s

Men and women were separated when they entered St John's Workhouse in Wood Street. They trod the same ground that soldiers had marched on during the Napoleonic Wars (1799–1815) and the American War of Independence (1775–83), when the land was an army barracks.

The workhouse gate at St John's.

St John's Workhouse was built in Wood Street in 1837 and the entrance to the establishment can still be seen today, despite the recent housing development. Parish councils were responsible for running the workhouses until the Poor Law Amendment Act of 1834 came into force and the Board of Guardians was set up to run each area. The Chelmsford Board was appointed on 15 August 1835 and they held their first meeting in the Black Boy Inn.

There were a number of workhouses in the district, namely, the Chantry House at Danbury, one in Stock, situated in Workhouse Lane (now Common Lane.). There were others at Great. Baddow, Buttsbury, South Hanningfield, Writtle, Great and Little Waltham One of the oldest was in Writtle, which was built around 1717.

The workhouse in New Street, Chelmsford, went back to the beginning of the eighteenth century but was comparatively small, having only fourteen rooms. There had been almshouses on the site but they had become too costly to run and were demolished. The workhouse was built in their place. The parish appointed a board of trustees to supervise the work and provided the money to build it. It would appear from the records that soon after it was built there was an outbreak of smallpox in the parish and the workhouse took in and cared for the sick. If a working man became destitute because of illness, the board would not always put him and his family straight into the workhouse but would give him a shilling to help the family overcome the financial difficulties they faced.

To be admitted to the workhouse a person or family would have had to have lived in the district for two years. People dreaded going into these institutions because there was a stigma attached and society looked down on them as failures. Once in the workhouse the strong were expected to work, and that included children. Workers were paid between 3d and 5d per day depending on their skills but children were paid 1d per day. The inmate's

Above left: The site of St John's today, which is now a housing estate.

Above right: Mildmay armshouse, 2013.

Chelmsford and Essex Hospital.

day started with breakfast, which normally consisted of porridge. They were not fed again until the task they had been set was finished. Three times a week they received meat and a pudding. Bearing in mind that the water supply was contaminated they were allocated 9 gallons of beer a week. Once a week they were deloused and given a change of clothing. The workhouse could take up to fifty people, including the master and his family.

Chelmsford and Essex Hospital

In 1818, long before there was a National Health Service, Chelmsford had a dispensary for the poor where the doctors and surgeons gave their services for free. The clinic was set up originally in Moulsham Street, next to a public house, but the building was so cramped and unsuitable that when there was a cholera outbreak, the authorities had to erect a tent in the grounds to accommodate the additional patients.

The popularity of the infirmary grew and people came from miles around to use the facilities. It became very overcrowded and it did have the added inconvenience of being next to a public house. It was decided that something had to be done and so the Infirmary Committee was set up and met in July 1880 to resolve the situation. After much debate it was decided to build a people's hospital and fund it by public subscription. They started to raise funds under the presidency of the Lord Lieutenant of Essex, Thomas Trevor. Money came pouring in from all classes of citizen, from farmworkers, manufacturers, and high society. In two years they had raised £4,680, which was a great deal of money in those times.

With that sum of money, and with more coming in daily, the committee started to search for a suitable site to build on. After an extensive search, they settled on an area of land in London Road, between Chestnut Villas and the Baptist church. Plans were drawn up by different professionals, including doctors. The hospital was built in three years and was opened by the Countess of Warwick in 1883, but the committee had overspent its budget by £1,000 and needed £10,000 to keep it running. The committee set about raising the necessary money by selling light refreshments, holding fetes and even had collecting boxes on the wall outside the hospital, in churches and public buildings.

The hospital was a two-storey building that had an emergency ward, with four beds on one side for men and two on the other side for women. Upstairs there were twelve free beds and to help with finances they had two single rooms for private patients. The wards were named after people who had made large donations. The hospital was lit by gas and had a dispensary and a mortuary.

The hospital was taken over by the National Health Sevice in 1946. Once a cure for tuberculosis had been found, Broomfield became a general hospital and joined Chelmsford and Essex hospital to fight general illnesses. As Broomfield Hospital expanded, it was decided that Chelmsford and Essex Hospital should become a day clinic, and they provided an excellent service, screening women for cancer. The hospital eventually closed.

DID YOU KNOW THAT...?

The Saxon Way, Broomfield, was called that because an Anglo-Saxon burial ground was discovered there and the relics that were found there are now in the British museum.

Broomfield Hospital in 1940. (Copyright Broomfield Hospital)

Men Only

During the 1930s and '40s tuberculosis was rife and the Essex County Hospital (now known as Broomfield) was built to meet this crisis. The first person to run the hospital was Dr William Yell. Tuberculosis has been with man since time began. Traces of the disease have been found in Neolithic man, who lived 9,000 years ago. It has also been found in Egyptian mummies and many other ancient civilizations.

The cure for this deadly disease, before the drug Streptomycin was brought out in 1945, was plenty of fresh air, sunshine, rest and good food. To keep the costs down, a lot of the vegetables were grown in the hospital's grounds by some of the patients. It took between six months and four years to recover from the disease.

Essex County Hospital was designed to face south in order to receive the maximum amount of sunshine. The patients were put out on the balconies, even in the depths of winter, but the hospital only treated men.

After being confined to bed for anything up to four years, most patients suffered from boredom. The staff tried to relieve this by having picture shows on Friday nights and with as many as four patients clinging on to one bed, porters raced them down the corridors to

Broomfield Hospital today.

A drawing of King Edward VI Grammar School in Moulsham.

secure the best places in the hall for the shows. Once Streptomycin came into regular use, TB began to decline and gradually the hospital changed over to general practice. The hospital played its part in the Second World War as 156 beds were allocated to wounded servicemen.

Women were not admitted until 1959, when one of the first women gave birth in the maternity ward. Over the years the hospital has given excellent service to the community and now covers most branches of medicine but one ward is still retained for chest infections.

DID YOU KNOW THAT...?

The Radcliff family originally owned the estate on which Broomfield Hospital stands and built a mansion house called Little Dumplings in 1904. The daughter, Constance, sold it to Essex County Council in order for the hospital to be built and work started two years before the Second World War. Amazingly the cost to build the original building was under £30,000, which is a lot less than what some of the extensions must have cost today.

The Oldest Schools in Chelmsford

King Edward VI

A royal warrant established the King Edward VI Grammar School in 1551. It was originally housed in the Old Friary in Moulsham Street until 1627. It was supervised by Sir Walter Mildmay, Sir Tyrell and Sir William Petre, and subsequently their descendents.

In 1678 one of Sir William's descendents was incarcerated in the Tower of London for being involved in a Popish plot. The school was originally set up to educate boys from Chelmsford and Moulsham in classical languages and the Anglican religion. It was funded by rents from a number of farms in the area, such as Hatfield Peverel, Tilbury and cottages in Great Baddow. Unfortunately, this only covered the cost of teaching religion and classics. The running of the school, i.e. heating, candles, books and maintenance of the building, had to be paid for by the students.

For the next 302 years it ran with one or two hiccups. In 1853, a dispute erupted over the curriculum and the school was closed for three years. The Victorians did not like what the Tudors had taught. The only way to change the curriculum was to bring in an Act of Parliament, but the school had insufficient money to finance a bill. Finally, parliament set up a Royal Commission in1860, which eventually resulted in The Endowed Schools Act in 1869. This allowed the schools to teach more modern subjects (a change from classics) and for the school to increase the number of students attending it.

Through the years the governors found financing the school difficult and it was necessary to sell off the farms and cottages. Luckily in 1944 the Education Act was passed and education became free to all, but they still had to sell the last cottage in 1957 to fund a school project.

The school moved to its present location in Broomfield Road under the guidance of Frank Rodgers, who became headmaster in 1885. After the First World War there was an increase in student numbers and so extensions were built to accommodate the additional children.

Famous People Educated at the School:
Lord Fowler, Conservative member of parliament and cabinet minister; Joseph Strutt, author of *Sports and Pastimes of the People of England*; Peter Joslin QPM, chief constable of Warwickshire police from (1983–98); Brian Parkyn, Labour MP; Clive Young, Bishop of Dunwich, Peter Seabrook, gardener; and Wing Commander Wilf Sizer of 213 Squadron.

Belgian Immigrants 1799, New Hall School

After the French Revolution the Roman Catholic nuns of the Holy Sepulchre were driven out of Liege and emigrated to England. There they set up the girls' school at New Hall in

King Edward VI today.

Drawing of Beaulieu in 1660, which later became New Hall School. (Copyright New Hall School)

1799. The history of New Hall goes back far beyond that date and first appears in the records in 1062, when the estate was granted to the canon of Waltham Abbey. Over the centuries it had a number of owners, but in 1516 Henry VIII bought it and spent £17,000 on building Beaulieu Palace. For a while, in 1527, England was governed from the palace when Henry stopped there on one of his frequent journeys round England.

It is understood that he started to plan his disposal of Katherine of Aragon and his marriage to Anne Boleyn at Beaulieu. Mary, Henry's daughter by Katherine and future Queen of England, lived in the palace for a time, but once Henry divorced Katherine he banned his daughter Mary from occupying it. Later, he relented when he made her godmother to his son Edward. Not everything went the king's way: fire broke out in the palace causing extensive damage, and Henry had to rebuild part of it.

The 3rd Earl of Sussex was granted the palace by Elizabeth I after her sister's death, and he carried out some building to the north wing. After over 400 years, Queen Elizabeth's coat of arms can still be seen reigning over the main entrance of the hall. Around 1653 Oliver Cromwell, who was made Lord Protector after the Civil War, decided he would like Beaulieu and purchased it for the grand sum of 5s. Not long after Oliver Cromwell died the Duke of Buckingham took over the palace and ironically entertained Charles II there when he was restored to the throne in 1660, after having been invited back. The building gradually deteriorated over the next seventy-seven years until finally some of it had to be demolished and rebuilt.

The school originally only catered for girls, but in 2005 the first boys were admitted. Today some boys and girls are boarders and others are day students. It is the only independent Catholic school in the area, with wonderful facilities, and is also one of the largest in the country.

New Hall School, 1900. (Copyright New Hall School)

Famous People Educated at the School:
Wildlife filmmaker Cindy Buxton, fashion designer Anya Hindmarch, journalist Felicity Landon and the racing driver Amanda Stretton.

Writtle College

Part of Writtle College is built on an old site of a palace that King John (1166–1216) owned. The college was established in 1893 and came about because of the drinking laws at that time. Parliament decided that because of the heavy drinking of the public, some alehouses, particularly in the poorer areas, should be closed. There was public outcry but the Conservative Party, under the leadership of Robert Cecil, Marquess of Salisbury, imposed a tax on alcohol and proposed to give it to the already wealthy brewers to compensate them for closing their public houses. The public again protested but the tax had raised more money than was needed for the compensation, so they decided to spend it on education. Some of the money was spent on establishing Writtle College.

Writtle College was originally housed in the premises previously occupied by King Edward VI Grammar School in Duke Street. It gradually outgrew the site and in 1940, a year into the war, it moved to its present position in Writtle. It is claimed that it is the largest college teaching agriculture and covers not only agriculture but engineering, horticultural, science, management and extra mural studies. The college covers over 150 hectares.

Chelmsford County High School for Girls

The school started with only seventy-six students in 1906, under headmistress Mabel Harcourt. Originally the girls had to be between twelve and eighteen years. A preparatory school was established for girls of eight, but this was discontinued in 1947. The school had only one male member of staff, Alfred Bamford.

In view of the poor transport conditions in the area, in 1910 the school decided to provide accommodation for girls who had to travel a long way and so acquired No. 39 Broomfield Road. By 1936 public transport had improved and so the governors decided to close the house down. At that time few girls went to university, but in 1916 one of its pupils, Winifred Picking, gained a first at Girton College, Cambridge.

During the First World War the school hosted Belgian pupils who had come to escape the horrors taking place in their country. In those far-off days the school had no shelters and so, during Zeppelin and bomber raids, the girls were given places to crouch down, away from windows and outside walls. Luckily, the practice never had to be used. During the Second World War the school was damaged on a number of occasions and had its windows blown out. Fortunately at the time the girls were on holiday.

Over the years there have been many changes to this excellent school, which is one of the highest achieving in the country.

The school has had some outstanding students over the years whose careers have ranged from MPs, to writers and sculptors.

Writtle College today.

Chelmsford County High School for Girls. (Copyright Chelmsford Girls County High School)

Chelmsford County High School for Girls today.

Anglia Ruskin University.

Famous People Educated at the School:
Dame Margaret Anstee, Under Secretary General, 1987; Karen Buck, MP for Regents Park and Kensington North; Anne Cullen, actress; Rachel Elnaugh, panelist on *Dragon's Den*; Sarah Perry, writer; and Catharini Stern, sculptor.

Anglia Ruskin University

Chelmsford's part of Anglia Ruskin University is close to the site of Bishop's Hall Mill, Mill House, and partly on the site that Hoffman's Ballbearing Factory occupied. Bishops Hall Mill and Bishops House were owned by the Bishop of London, who also owned the Manor of Chelmsford. William de-Sainte-Mere- Eglise was bishop between 1051 and 1075. Both Bishops Hall and the Mill were mentioned in the Doomsday Book.

Henry VIII took over both properties during the Dissolution of the Monasteries. In 1563 Thomas Mildmay purchased the Manor of Chelmsford and it remained in the family until 1917. The mill was occupied by the Marriage family in 1795 and they used it for grinding corn. Their firm is still going strong today.

It is thought that Anne Knight was born in a property where part of the Anglia Ruskin University stands. She was born in 1787 into a Quaker family. She was a leading light in the Anti-Slavery Movement and the Women's Rights Movement and organized public meetings for both.

Miscellany

Chelmsford Museum

It is difficult to believe that the very sophisticated Chelmsford Museum started off in the front room of the first governor of Springfield Prison, Capt. T. C. Neal. He belonged to the Chelmsford Philosophical Society, and by 1843 the items they had collected had outgrown his front room. They were forced to look for alternative accommodation and acquired a building in Museum Terrace. In time they moved to Oaklands House, which was originally owned by the Abbot of Westminster. Alderman Wells then purchased it in 1866. He was a rich local brewer and coal merchant who needed a larger house for his growing family. The house was named after an oak tree which had been in the grounds for hundreds of years until it was blown down in the storm of 1987.

In 1930 Chelmsford Council bought the house and the museum has been there ever since. It has a wonderful exhibition of some of the industries of the city, including firms such as Marconi, Crompton and Hoffman's. There are working models, a favorite of which is the glass beehive where bees can be seen coming and going as they gather nectar and make honey.

One of the rooms is delegated to the Essex Regiments and has a wonderful exhibition of military items.

In the well-kept gardens is the cannon that was captured from the Russians during the Battle of Sevastopol during the Crimean War (1853–56). It used to stand outside Shire Hall but was moved after some youths tried to fire it – luckily without a cannonball, or else the Saracen's Head would have been demolished.   .

In the Essex Regiment rooms is one of the prized exhibits of the Museum: a French Eagle taken off a French soldier during the battle of Salamanca during the wars with Napoleon in 1812.

Bishop's Hall Mill

Bishop's Hall Mill was mentioned in the Doomsday Book of 1086 and was owned by William the Bishop of London. The mill, the mill house and the rectory were taken over by Henry VIII during the Dissolution of the Monasteries, 1536–41 following the Act of Supremacy in 1534, when he was made head of the Church of England. It was estimated that one in fifty men was in religious orders at that time.

Henry carried out the Dissolution of the Monasteries to increase his income and partially fund his war with France in 1539. After Henry's death in 1547, he was succeeded by Edward VI, who was only nine when he became King and ruled for only six years. He was succeeded by Bloody Mary, who restored the Catholic faith to England. She reigned until 1558, when

The museum (Oak House) during the 1930s.

The Chelmsford Museum today.

Painting of Bishop's Hall in its heyday.

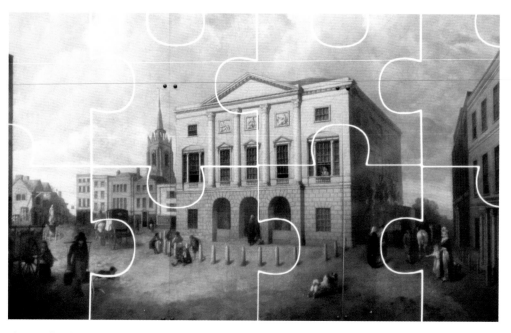

Shire Hall, where many famous trials were held.

Queen Elizabeth came to the throne. Her auditor, Thomas Mildmay, purchased the Manor of Chelmsford in 1563 and it remained in the family until 1917.

Hoffmann's took over the land and the surrounding area and built their ball-bearing factory. They were an offshoot of an American company owned by Gustav Hoffmann, who enabled Charles and Geoffrey Barrett to set up the English company that manufactured ball-bearings used for all types of machinery, including aircraft. Needless to say the factory was bombed by the Germans during both world wars. At one time it employed over 7,500 people. After being taken over a number of times the company was finally purchased by a Japanese firm and moved to Newark-on-Trent. Most of the factory was demolished in 1990 and became part of Anglia Ruskin University.

A Staircase that Killed

Over the centuries the Shire Hall has seen many court cases, but none so dramatic as in 1856 when four men were put on trial for shooting and killing William Hales, a gamekeeper who worked for Sir John Tyrell of Boreham House. Mr Hales caught the gang poaching. When he tried to stop them one lost his nerve and blasted Mr Hales with his shotgun, killing him. The citizens of Chelmsford were incensed by the murder of a very popular family man and set up a fund for his widow and children. Everyone was out to catch the poachers and they were finally caught and put on trial.

The hearing was held in one of the upper rooms at Shire Hall. The small courtroom soon became full to the brim and people were still trying to climb the staircase. Soon the small courtroom was bursting at the seams but still people continued to try and climb the stairs, pushing and shoving each other, hoping to see the trial. Suddenly, there was a loud crack and people looked at one another in fear. Then the staircase collapsed and they found they were tumbling down on top of one another. People clung to the railings for dear life while others tried to stop themselves tumbling down to the floor below. Master Moss, a boy of eighteen, stood below the falling staircase and was crushed to death; a number of people were badly injured. The judge, audience, prisoners and prison officers were stranded in midair and had no way of getting down. In the end, somebody brought a ladder and everybody slowly climbed down, step-by-step, to the ground floor. Soon the trial was resumed in another room, where everyone expected the judge to pronounce the death sentence, but he surprised everybody by ordering the prisoners to be transported to Australia. They served only part of their sentence and returned to England after a few years.

The witch trials of the late sixteenth century were held in the courthouse prior to Shire Hall being built in its place. It was called Tudor Market Place or sometimes Great Cross. The witch trials were instigated by the Witch Finder, Gen. Matthew Hopkins, who was responsible for the deaths of 230 so-called witches.

One of the worst cases was when three witches were hanged on the evidence of a twelve-year-old child. Agnes Waterhouse, her daughter Joan and an Elizabeth Francis were accused of having a cat which helped them cast spells. The cat, it was alleged, had an ape's head and horns. They were accused of causing the death of a man and his cows. They were also accused of turning his butter and cheese rancid.

In 1789 the old building was condemned and the County Surveyor, Mr Johnson, was given the task of building Shire Hall. It took two years to build and cost £14,000, paid for by the ratepayers. To store the construction material the builders hired a field in Duke Street. On the outside of Shire Hall there are three figures representing mercy, wisdom and justice. The road outside the Hall became a quagmire during the winter, especially because of the horse and carriage traffic. During the summer it was the reverse and became a dust bowl.

The cannon that now stands in the grounds of the museum once stood outside the Hall. It was subjected to pranks by the local youths, who one day went too far and loaded the artillery piece with gun powder and standing back, fired it. Luckily, they did not have a cannon ball in the barrel or the Saracen's Head might today just be called the Saracen. The gun was originally brought back from the Crimean War after the battle of Sevastopol in 1854.

DID YOU KNOW THAT...?

There was a skating rink in Chelmsford before the leisure centre opened.

Regency Cinema

Very few of the old cinemas have survived. Most have gone through several transitions before being completely redeveloped. We are lucky in Chelmsford because the façade of the Regent Cinema remains intact. Although the interior has been converted into a public house, it still has many of its original features.

It was originally built in 1913 and the foyer was rebuilt in 1935, no doubt to accommodate the increase in attendance for the new developing industry of the cinema, when most families went to the pictures at least once a week. In its heyday it could seat 1,000 people.

Most people of my age will remember the Saturday-morning pictures and the excitement it engendered, especially when the hero came on and a cheer went up, as opposed to the hisses when the villain appeared. It is said that the building is haunted and an investigation was carried out to find out about the ghost. A Ouija board was used and to everybody's embarrassment it was found that the ghost was the morning cleaner!

In 1975 it was converted to a bingo hall, which closed in 1993, but it is now a thriving public house.

The skating rink, 1906.

The Regency Cinema today.

Acknowledgements

I wish to express my thanks to the following people, without whose help and patience this book would never have been written. Although I have made every effort to be as accurate as possible, any mistakes are mine and I apologise in advance for them.

First, I must thank my friend Olive Norfolk for her help in research but who sadly passed away on the 16 November 2014. My good friend Sylvia Kent who has given me so much help. The staff at the Chelmsford Museum, especially Dr Mark Curteis PhD. AMA FRNs for his invaluable help. Becky, Mick Berry and the team at Essex Police Museum, which is well worth a visit on a Saturday. I wish to thank Lindsey Thompson PR and Marketing Manager of King Edward VI Grammar School, Liz Meer of Gray & Sons, Brewers, and Becky the waitress at the Angel public house. A special thank you to Chris Cocks, Jenny Stephens and Phil Clement at Amberley Publishing.

There is one person who has shown me patience and understanding while writing this book, and whose editing skills I could not do without: Joan my wife, without whose help this book would never have been written.